TOM   M

2023

A BOOK OF
GRACE-FILLED
DAYS

LOYOLAPRESS.
A JESUIT MINISTRY

Chicago

LOYOLA PRESS.
A JESUIT MINISTRY

www.loyolapress.com

© 2022 Loyola Press
All rights reserved.

Scripture excerpts are taken from the *Lectionary for Mass for Use in the Dioceses of the United States of America, second typical edition*, Copyright 2001, 1998, 1997, 1986, 1970 by the Confraternity of Christian Doctrine, Washington, DC. Used with permission. All rights reserved. No part of the *Lectionary for Mass* may be reproduced in any form without permission in writing from the copyright owner.

Cover and interior design by Kathy Kikkert.

ISBN: 978-0-8294-5454-3
Library of Congress Control Number: 2022936246

Printed in the United States of America.
22 23 24 25 26 27 28 29 30 31 Versa 10 9 8 7 6 5 4 3 2 1a

INTRODUCTION

During the year I spent reflecting on the daily Scripture passages for this book, I came to see that the Bible is not a collection of "thou shalt nots," as many suspect, so much as it is a steady outpouring of personal invitations and clues on how to experience union with a loving God. In my reflections I found myself highlighting these invitations, usually in the form of a key word or phrase that grabbed my attention and focused my response. The Scriptures, Old and New Testaments alike, are full of such clues and urgings, like

- **Stay Awake**: Something wonderful and important is about to happen.
- **Behold**: Jesus used this word as an alert that a divine manifestation was at hand.

- **Ponder**: Mary teaches us the value of pondering, which is not the same as thinking things through. It's more a matter of absorbing the deep truths woven throughout our lives.
- **Prepare**: The soil must be prepared for the seed that is about to be sown.
- **Be not afraid**: This is Jesus' most repeated phrase in the Gospels. Fear blocks the coming of the Kingdom in our hearts.
- **Empty yourself**: Thy Kingdom come, my kingdom go.
- **Learn from the Pharisees**: Polish the inside, not the outside, of your cup.
- **Come work in the Vineyard**: He said to them, "The harvest is abundant but the laborers are few; so ask the master of the harvest to send out laborers for his harvest." Luke 10:2
- **Embrace paradox**: "Amen, amen, I say to you, unless a grain of wheat falls to the ground and dies, it remains just a grain of wheat; but if it dies, it produces much fruit." John 12:24
- **Rejoice**: We must receive with joy the startling truth of resurrection if we are to fully follow Jesus.

My goal has been to help you (and myself) recognize how our individual life stories are connected to God's grand story of Creation and salvation, giving us meaning and purpose and leading us to abundant life. Coming to faith is a matter of having eyes to see, ears to hear, and a heart that's willing. Daily practice of encountering God in the Scriptures has the power to heal us, ground us in God's grace, and inspire us to be channels of God's love to the world. I will be praying for you throughout the coming year that the words of Scripture will fall on rich soil in your mind, heart, body, and actions and bring forth great fruit—just by you being your best self in the life you are called to. If you approach these daily readings with a generous and willing heart, God will surely bless you with strength, healing, and abundant joy.

Tom McGrath

So too, you also must be prepared,
for at an hour you do not expect,
the Son of Man will come.
—MATTHEW 24:44

"Be prepared!" says Jesus. Advent is the time to prepare for the coming of Jesus. But how? The context of today's reading indicates that awareness and inner vigilance are key. I asked friends what practices they use to stay vigilant during Advent. One said, "My family and I light the Advent wreath each night before dinner." Another said, "I sit quietly with just the Christmas lights on, remembering Christmases past." Yet another said, "When I take my dog for a walk, I quietly hum Advent and Christmas hymns to her." Light a candle, recall the days of yore, let the hymns of the season wash over you. How would you answer my question?

Isaiah 2:1–5
Psalm 122:1–2,3–4,4–5,6–7,8–9
Romans 13:11–14
Matthew 24:37–44

NOVEMBER 28

For over all, the LORD's glory will be shelter
and protection:
shade from the parching heat of day,
refuge and cover from storm and rain.
—ISAIAH 4:6

Many Advent readings reveal what to expect when the Son of God arrives. Today's prophetic words from Isaiah declare that God will provide shelter and protection—relief from the parching heat and cover from storm and rain. Isaiah shows up a lot in Advent and Lent because his prophetic vision reveals so much about our human longing and about the divine response. His words were powerful in his day, just as they were relevant to Jesus' age and are no less revelatory in ours.

We sense that once there was a time of no separation between ourselves and God, and we long to find a way back. Jesus is coming.

Isaiah 4:2–6
Psalm 122:1–2,3–4b,4cd–5,6–7,8–9
Matthew 8:5–11

Tuesday

NOVEMBER 29

*Not by appearance shall he judge,
nor by hearsay shall he decide,
But he shall judge the poor with justice,
and decide aright for the land's afflicted.*
—ISAIAH 11:3–4

"That's not fair!" is a common complaint. It's heard out on the
playground as well as at the watercooler, in City Hall, and
around the family table. We want to be treated justly, which
means we each want to be seen as a person of dignity. God
not only sees us as people of dignity but also conferred that
dignity upon us. One sign of the coming of the Lord is that
all people, even the poor and afflicted who typically get
overlooked, will receive justice and be treated as royalty.
May it be so!

Isaiah 11:1–10
Psalm 72:1–2,7–8,12–13,17
Luke 10:21–24

⇒ 3 ⇐

But how can they call on him in whom they
have not believed?
And how can they believe in him of whom
they have not heard?
—ROMANS 10:14

Pastors and directors of religious education take St. Paul's questions to heart. They put a lot of creativity into fashioning effective responses. How can we pass on a two-thousand-year-old tradition in a way that resonates in the hearts of those we encounter—especially the young? After all, we want children not only to know *about* God but also to be able to "taste and see the goodness of the Lord." St. Paul and the other apostles gave witness to God by their words and deeds. They lived the faith so that others could see and be likewise moved to belief. Be on the lookout for one opportunity to witness to your faith today.

Romans 10:9–18
Psalm 19:8,9,10,11
Matthew 4:18–22

Thursday

DECEMBER 1

It is better to take refuge in the LORD
than to trust in man.
It is better to take refuge in the LORD
than to trust in princes.
—PSALM 118:8–9

Today's readings combine to deliver a focused message. The Gospel says build your house (life) on rock. The opening reading urges, "Trust in the Lord forever! / For the Lord is an eternal Rock." And the psalm puts a fine point on it, telling us in whom our trust belongs. It's fine to be trust-ready. In fact, wisely trusting others is an essential quality of the kingdom. But the authors of all three readings know the danger of treating as God that which is not God: money, popularity, power. The list is endless. Pray today: God, help me see where I edge you out of first place in my mind and heart.

Isaiah 26:1–6
Psalm 118:1 and 8–9,19–21,25–27a
Matthew 7:21,24–27

DECEMBER 2

One thing I ask of the LORD;
this I seek:
To dwell in the house of the LORD
all the days of my life.
—PSALM 27:4

"D-a-a-a-d, why do I have to be home by curfew?" To which Dad responds, "My house, my rules." Which makes me suspect that today's psalm excerpt is not high on the list of most teenagers. To dwell in the house of the Lord means to live according to God's will (the biblical version of "my house, my rules"). It takes spiritual maturity to recognize that the divine will is *for* us, not against us. God's desire is that we experience the fullness of life in Christ, in whom we find our true home.

Isaiah 29:17–24
Psalm 27:1,4,13–14
Matthew 9:27–31

⇒ 6 ⇐

DECEMBER 3

• ST. FRANCIS XAVIER, PRIEST •

*Without cost you have received; without cost you are
to give.*
—MATTHEW 10:8

Christmas is coming, and it's a time to give gifts. But Advent
is also a time to give gifts—the gifts you have been given
rather than the gifts you buy. What gifts do you have? I'll bet
there are some you're not even aware of. The gifts God gives
us are meant for the good of the world, including those who
are closest to us. Today, consider giving the gift of
thoughtfulness to people you encounter: write a note of
encouragement to someone going through a rough time; stop
what you're doing when a family member or coworker asks a
question, look him or her in the eye, and give your full
attention. Every interaction offers another chance to give a
gift you've been given: your time, your attention, your care.

Isaiah 30:19–21,23–26
Psalm 147:1–2,3–4,5–6
Matthew 9:35—10:1,5a,6–8

Sunday

DECEMBER 4

SECOND SUNDAY OF ADVENT •

At that time Jerusalem, all Judea,
and the whole region around the Jordan
were going out to him
and were being baptized by him in the Jordan River
as they acknowledged their sins.
—MATTHEW 3:5–6

John the Baptist preached repentance, crying, "Prepare the
way of the Lord." He was calling for a change of mind as
evidenced in a change of people's behavior through the
acknowledgment of their sins. Why did so many people heed
the harshness of his call and come to the desert to repent and
be baptized? There is a promise in repentance. It's the
promise of escaping the illusions and delusions our minds
play on us, which leave us "polishing the outside of the cup,"
as Jesus later preached, and instead taking up the hard work
of interior change. Prepare!

Isaiah 11:1–10
Psalm 72:1–2,7–8,12–13,17
Romans 15:4–9
Matthew 3:1–12

8 ⇐

Streams will burst forth in the desert,
and rivers in the steppe.
The burning sands will become pools,
and the thirsty ground, springs of water.
—ISAIAH 35:6–7

Isaiah often uses nature images to convey spiritual messages.
His prophecies offer imagery to contemplate that reveal
God's wishes for how we can thrive. All of creation is
connected. What is outside can be the entrée to the inside if
we turn off the judgments and approach with open minds
and expectant hearts. In today's verse Isaiah uses the symbol
of water transforming dry and barren land. Where is the
desert in your life lately? What part of your life yearns for
rivers and streams to burst forth so that burning sands can
become pools of refreshing water?

Isaiah 35:1–10
Psalm 85:9ab and 10,11–12,13–14
Luke 5:17–26

All flesh is grass,
and all their glory like the flower of the field.
The grass withers and the flower wilts.
—ISAIAH 40:6–7

In most spiritual traditions, facing one's mortality is a sobering necessity if any real progress is to be made. If we can face the hard truth of our inevitable death, then we can be consoled by the flip side of the paradox: we are cherished by God. If we can hold both these truths in our hearts (for it takes the grace of God to both see our mortality and experience our preciousness in God's eyes), we can live in right relationship with the God who creates us, redeems us, and sets us free to live this day in peace and generous love.

Isaiah 40:1–11
Psalm 96:1–2,3 and 10ac,11–12,13
Matthew 18:12–14

DECEMBER 7

• ST. AMBROSE, BISHOP AND DOCTOR OF THE CHURCH •

Jesus said to the crowds:
"Come to me, all you who labor and are burdened,
and I will give you rest."
—MATTHEW 11:28

First of all, Jesus is speaking to everyone, not just to his disciples. That means he is speaking to you. He says, "I will give you rest." Let that sink in. What will free you of your burdens is to turn your worries over to God in confidence and simply do the next right thing in front of you. It sounds too simple to be true, but try it for today. Bundle all your burdens and place them in God's lap. Breathe. Listen for the still, small voice inside to guide you and finish one task, answer one text, say one prayer. He will give you rest.

Isaiah 40:25–31
Psalm 103:1–2,3–4,8 and 10
Matthew 11:28–30

Thursday

DECEMBER 8

• THE IMMACULATE CONCEPTION OF THE BLESSED VIRGIN MARY (PATRONAL
FEAST DAY OF THE UNITED STATES OF AMERICA) •

He answered, "I heard you in the garden;
but I was afraid, because I was naked,
so I hid myself."
Then [God] asked, "Who told you that you were naked?"
—GENESIS 3:10–11

One day Adam and Eve walk freely with God in the garden,
and all is well. The next day, they hide from God, ashamed of
who they are. "Who told you that you were naked?" asks God.
Their innocence now lost, their sense of their own worthiness
comes into question. In German, the word for this loss means
"inherited wound." We know it as original sin. Today,
contemplate Mary, who was conceived without that inherited
wound. Her yes to God opened the door for the grace we need
to transcend the effects of sin and live anew in Christ.

Genesis 3:9–15,20
Psalm 98:1,2–3ab,3cd–4
Ephesians 1:3–6,11–12
Luke 1:26–38

⇒ 12 ⇐

Friday

DECEMBER 9

He is like a tree
planted near running water,
That yields its fruit in due season,
and whose leaves never fade.
—PSALM 1:3

Are you planted well? Are there sources of grace around you that help you yield good fruit in your life and work, or are your leaves beginning to fade? One place to check is the media you consume. Is it uplifting? Inspiring, even? Or does it leave you irritated, agitated, and leaning toward despair? Psalm 1 begins, "Blessed is the man who follows not / the counsel of the wicked." Be sure the counsel that comes your way in the form of your media choices is life-giving, calling out the best in you. No one ought to live beside a polluted stream.

Isaiah 48:17–19
Psalm 1:1–2,3,4 and 6
Matthew 11:16–19

DECEMBER 10

In those days,
like a fire there appeared the prophet Elijah
whose words were as a flaming furnace.
—SIRACH 48:1

Elijah, the prophet, knew how to make an entrance, and an even flashier exit. He was taken aloft on a chariot—with fiery horses, no less! He looms large in biblical history, and it was thought in Jesus' time that Elijah would reappear before the Messiah would come. And he did, in a sense, because John the Baptist was thought to carry the spirit of Elijah, delivering his own words urging repentance "like a flaming furnace." Sometimes it takes a jolt out of the blue to get our attention. Yet, even when we've drifted off course, God will find a way. How is God trying to reach you today?

Sirach 48:1–4,9–11
Psalm 80:2ac and 3b,15–16,18–19
Matthew 17:9a,10–13

DECEMBER 11

• THIRD SUNDAY OF ADVENT •

When John the Baptist heard in prison of the works
of the Christ,
he sent his disciples to Jesus with this question,
"Are you the one who is to come,
or should we look for another?"
—MATTHEW 11:2–3

Jesus responded to the Baptist's question not by claiming a title but by pointing to the fruits of his efforts: the blind see, the lame walk, lepers are cleansed, the deaf hear. . . . John's vision leaned toward judgment and vindication. Jesus' efforts were all about reconciliation and restoration. Vindication is appealing, but our deepest desire is that we be restored to the state of communion that existed before the fall of Adam and Eve. Even now, instead of judgment, Jesus offers wholeness. Is that what you've been looking for?

Isaiah 35:1–6a,10
Psalm 146:6–7,8–9,9–10
James 5:7–10
Matthew 11:2–11

DECEMBER 12

• OUR LADY OF GUADALUPE •

*A great sign appeared in the sky, a woman clothed
with the sun.*
—REVELATION 12:1

Everyone wants to be seen and blessed. We want that from
our parents, friends, coworkers, and God. Our Lady of
Guadalupe saw a poor man called Juan Diego and blessed
him with a mission: convince the bishop to build a church on
that spot. The bishop was skeptical. Juan Diego feared he
had let the Lady down and attempted to hide from her on his
way to help his dying uncle. She forever won the hearts of
the indigenous people when, offering her help, in his original
language, she said, "Am I not here, I who am your mother?"
Millions of indigenous people became Catholic shortly
thereafter, and devotion to Our Lady of Guadalupe remains
strong. She is here for you, too.

Zechariah 2:14–17 or Revelation 11:19a; 12:1–6a,10ab
Judith 13:18bcde,19
Luke 1:26–38 or 1:39–47

DECEMBER 13

• ST. LUCY, VIRGIN AND MARTYR •

The LORD is close to the brokenhearted;
and those who are crushed in spirit he saves.
—PSALM 34:19

Some people have a hard time during the Christmas season. Society's expectation that everyone should be happy and celebratory is an added burden when you are already brokenhearted or crushed in spirit. Advent offers a number of practices to offset the demand to be jolly. Light a candle, or preferably an Advent wreath, and pray or sing, "O Come, O Come, Emmanuel," a song of great expectation that Christ will come and save us. Another practice is to read from the Psalms, which include psalms on every human emotion, including feeling lost and alone. Finally, find a safe person with whom you can talk honestly about your feelings. God works for our good in many ways.

Zephaniah 3:1–2,9–13
Psalm 34:2–3,6–7,17–18,19 and 23
Matthew 21:28–32

DECEMBER 14

• ST. JOHN OF THE CROSS, PRIEST AND DOCTOR OF THE CHURCH •

I am the LORD, there is no other;
I form the light, and create the darkness.
—ISAIAH 45:6–7

Today is the feast of St. John of the Cross, most known for his classic spiritual poem *Dark Night of the Soul*. Many spiritual seekers experience a Dark Night as they progress on their spiritual path. Early on along the path we can experience great consolation as we taste and see the goodness of the Lord. But often, then the early consolation fades and a spiritual darkness sets in. As Bishop Robert Barron says, "The darkness, too, comes from God, because we're not meant to fall in love with the consolation, we're meant to fall in love with God." Don't fear the darkness. As your sight becomes accustomed, you're bound to see a skyful of stars.

Isaiah 45:6c–8,18,21c–25
Psalm 85:9ab and 10,11–12,13–14
Luke 7:18b–23

DECEMBER 15

Behold, I am sending my messenger ahead of you,
he will prepare your way before you.
—LUKE 7:27

John the Baptist must have been an extraordinary presence.
He attracted large crowds to the desert with his challenge to
repent. He sparked a flame of desire in those who confessed
their sins, and a hunger for God in those who came forward
to be baptized. Who in your life, now or in the past, sparks
the flame of desire for God in you? As you prepare this
Advent for the coming of Jesus, be mindful of those who
nurture that hunger in person or in memory.

Isaiah 54:1–10
Psalm 30:2 and 4,5–6,11–12a and 13b
Luke 7:24–30

Blessed is the man who does this,
the son of man who holds to it;
Who keeps the sabbath free from profanation,
and his hand from any evildoing.
—ISAIAH 56:2

Keeping holy the Sabbath is a bedrock practice of Jewish
believers. There are two elements involved in keeping
Sabbath: remembering its purpose and observing its customs
and restrictions. Both these considerations reinforce two
defining events in the relationship between God and the
chosen people: (1) after creating Adam and Eve, God rested on
the seventh day, and (2) God rescued the Jewish people from
slavery in Egypt. Observing the Sabbath is a requirement of
Christians, too. It's a chance to renounce unhealthy
attachment to work and self-reliance (thinking we can be
self-made saints) and to accept the delights that God provides
in the form of rest, refreshment, and sustaining relationships.

Isaiah 56:1–3a,6–8
Psalm 67:2–3,5,7–8
John 5:33–36

Saturday

DECEMBER 17

*The book of the genealogy of Jesus Christ,
the son of David, the son of Abraham.*
—MATTHEW 1:1

It's a curious assortment of people who show up in the
genealogy of Jesus as recorded in the Gospel of Matthew.
The list includes many ne'er-do-wells while excluding some
exemplary models of holiness from Jewish history. A
significant number are notorious for scandalous situations
they were involved in—or caused. And some would be
considered relative nobodies, their identities lost to history.
These last are the people who speak to me most. Though
they may not have had great accomplishments and flew
mostly under the radar, they played their part by just
showing up and living their lives. I relate to that. We all
belong. We all play our part. God is the author of this story,
and I'm just grateful to be here.

Genesis 49:2,8–10
Psalm 72:1–2,3–4ab,7–8,17
Matthew 1:1–17

DECEMBER 18

• FOURTH SUNDAY OF ADVENT •

The angel of the Lord appeared to him in a dream
and said,
"Joseph, son of David,
do not be afraid to take Mary your wife into your home.
For it is through the Holy Spirit
that this child has been conceived in her."
—MATTHEW 1:20

Note what can happen when the reign of God is announced. Moved by love, Joseph decides to protect Mary from scandal and shame. With that on his mind, Joseph responds to grace by paying attention to his dream in which he learns God's amazing plans. When he wakes up, he wastes no time and takes Mary into his home. Joseph, the carpenter, made space in his heart and in his home for the coming of our Lord, Jesus Christ. This week, let us do the same.

Isaiah 7:10–14
Psalm 24:1–2,3–4,5–6 (7c and 10b)
Romans 1:1–7
Matthew 1:18–24

DECEMBER 19

For you are my hope, O LORD;
my trust, O God, from my youth.
—PSALM 71:5

Advent is a season of hope, yet somewhere along the line it became a season of wishes. Wishes are specific and often transient. Hope runs deeper. One Christmas Eve, after a festive dinner with relatives, my wife, daughters, and I arrived home. After unloading the bags of gifts from the car, we all felt an emptiness. "Bundle up, we're going for a walk," announced my wife. As we stepped out on the porch, snow began to fall—big fluffy flakes, falling like grace. We walked the streets of our neighborhood, transformed now by loveliness. "I feel like we're a tiny family walking in a snow globe," said one of my daughters. Yes, I thought. A snow globe being held in the hands of God.

Judges 13:2–7,24–25a
Psalm 71:3–4a,5–6ab,16–17
Luke 1:5–25

DECEMBER 20

But Mary said to the angel,
"How can this be,
since I have no relations with a man?"
—LUKE 1:34

Good question, Mary. How is it that a virgin becomes pregnant? I find it best to begin with the question "What happened?" instead of "How?" And what happened with the birth of Jesus is that the Son of God, who existed from before time and through whom all things were made, became human and dwells among us—not just in the time of Herod but even now and always. And then we can ask why, which is the most important question. He came out of love for us, to reconcile all humanity with our Creator by the forgiveness of our sins and to bring us to everlasting life. This is not something for the brain alone to figure out but for the heart to receive, ponder, and recognize as true.

Isaiah 7:10–14
Psalm 24:1–2,3–4ab,5–6
Luke 1:26–38

DECEMBER 21

• ST. PETER CANISIUS, PRIEST AND DOCTOR OF THE CHURCH •

When Elizabeth heard Mary's greeting,
the infant leaped in her womb.
—LUKE 1:41

Mary traveled to the hill country in haste. Having received the news of her pregnancy, she rushed to the house of her cousin Elizabeth. When they met, the infant in Elizabeth's womb leapt for joy. Of all the Gospel accounts, this passage showcases to me Jesus' humanity the most. We receive our children even before they are born. They are already a reality in our lives as we prepare not just our homes but also our hearts and our extended families for the new arrival. Imagine yourself in this domestic scene as the cousins gather and greet one another with excitement and care. Let us join Mary and Elizabeth as they wait in joyful hope for the coming of our savior, Jesus Christ.

Song of Songs 2:8–14 or Zephaniah 3:14–18a
Psalm 33:2–3,11–12,20–21
Luke 1:39–45

Thursday

DECEMBER 22

Mary said:
"My soul proclaims the greatness of the Lord,
my spirit rejoices in God my savior."
—LUKE 1:46–47

Have you ever felt that way before? Mary perfectly captures in
words the experience of a heart overflowing with gratitude,
elation, and praise because of God's great love. The entire
prayer is a perfect one to pray when you're full of the love of
God—or when you're feeling quite the opposite. The prayer
captures a sense of the hope people held for what the Messiah
would bring: casting down the unjust mighty and lifting up the
lowly, filling up the hungry and sending the rich away empty.
Once again, the themes of justice and mercy rise up in
anticipation of Jesus. O come, O come, Emmanuel.

1 Samuel 1:24–28
1 Samuel 2:1,4–5,6–7,8abcd
Luke 1:46–56

Thus says the Lord GOD:
Lo, I am sending my messenger
to prepare the way before me.
—MALACHI 3:1

Who needs to be prepared? The people in darkness who long to see a great light, that's who. That was true in the age of Malachi, during the time of John the Baptist, and during our time as well. One secret and fun way to prepare is to watch a favorite Christmas movie or program—even (and especially) the ones aimed at kids. Just make sure it conveys the spirit of Christ—where love overcomes hate, where the rich, so blind to the plight of others, have their sight restored and their heart softened, where the least likely one becomes the hero who saves the day. These are more than mere sentiment; they are mini-homilies that proclaim the good news that the kingdom is already emerging in our midst.

Malachi 3:1–4,23–24
Psalm 25:4–5ab,8–9,10 and 14
Luke 1:57–66

DECEMBER 24

> *In the tender compassion of our God*
> *the dawn from on high shall break upon us,*
> *to shine on those who dwell in darkness*
> *and the shadow of death,*
> *and to guide our feet into the way of peace.*
> —LUKE 1:78–79

These closing words of Zechariah's canticle are, to me, the essence of what Christmas holds in store for us all. It is God's tender compassion that brings this moment—not anything we've earned or done. The dawn is breaking, bringing light and hope. We no longer need to live in the shadow of death because God has sent his Son to guide our feet on the way of peace—and eternal life. Merry Christmas, dear reader!

2 Samuel 7:1–5,8b–12,14a,16
Psalm 89:2–3,4–5,27 and 29
Luke 1:67–79

And this will be a sign for you:
you will find an infant wrapped in swaddling clothes
and lying in a manger.
—LUKE 2:12

While watching my granddaughter arrange the cast of characters in the manger—just so—I recalled my own fascination with this scene as a kid. A psychologist once told me the manger scene demands attention because it represents the whole cosmos. There's a star above, and angels. There are shepherds and kings, animals and hay, and a family. In the very center lies a little baby, so powerless, yet so powerful. It's all there. It all belongs. And there's a place for you.

VIGIL:	DAWN:
Isaiah 62:1–5	Isaiah 62:11–12
Psalm 89:4–5,16–17,27,29 (2a)	Psalm 97:1,6,11–12
Acts 13:16–17,22–25	Titus 3:4–7
Matthew 1:1–25 or 1:18–25	Luke 2:15–20
NIGHT:	DAY:
Isaiah 9:1–6	Isaiah 52:7–10
Psalm 96:1–2,2–3,11–12,13	Psalm 98:1,2–3,3–4,5–6 (3c)
Titus 2:11–14	Hebrews 1:1–6
Luke 2:1–14	John 1:1–18 or 1:1–5,9–14

DECEMBER 26

• ST. STEPHEN, THE FIRST MARTYR •

They threw him out of the city, and began to stone him.
The witnesses laid down their cloaks
at the feet of a young man named Saul.
—ACTS 7:58

I hope you had a Merry Christmas, because today we're focusing on martyrdom—St. Stephen, the first Christian martyr, as a matter of fact. He had been one of seven deacons appointed by the apostles to distribute food and charitable aid to poorer members of the community. He was known to be filled with grace and power, working great wonders and signs among the people. He fell afoul of Jewish leaders who saw his preaching about Jesus as blasphemy. He was unperturbed as he faced death. His last words were, "Lord Jesus, receive my spirit."

Acts 6:8–10; 7:54–59
Psalm 31:3cd–4,6 and 8ab,16bc and 17
Matthew 10:17–22

DECEMBER 27

• ST. JOHN, APOSTLE AND EVANGELIST •

Beloved:
What was from the beginning,
what we have heard,
what we have seen with our eyes,
what we looked upon
and touched with our hands
concerns the Word of life.
—1 JOHN 1:1

St. John the Evangelist makes it clear he was an eyewitness to
Jesus' life, death, and resurrection. He wrote elegantly what
he saw, heard, and came to believe. The opening to his
Gospel echoes the opening of the book of Genesis and is
breathtaking in its beauty and scope: "In the beginning was
the Word, and the Word was with God, and the Word was
God." At the end of today's reading he admits, "We are
writing this so that our joy may be complete." Some, such as
John, who encountered Jesus felt compelled to tell about
him, to our great benefit.

1 John 1:1–4
Psalm 97:1–2,5–6,11–12
John 20:1a,2–8

DECEMBER 28

• THE HOLY INNOCENTS, MARTYRS •

When Herod realized that he had been deceived
by the magi,
he became furious.
He ordered the massacre of all the boys in Bethlehem
and its vicinity
two years old and under.
—MATTHEW 2:13

Today's reading is an example of the danger inherent in
power. Infuriated by his failure to manipulate the Magi into
reporting on Jesus, Herod chose to use brutal violence to
eradicate a perceived threat to his coveted status. Jesus
modeled power differently by washing the apostles' feet. He
demonstrated that authority is meant to serve, not oppress.
Humility is not often associated with the idea of power, but
it's essential that it should be if we are to survive as a planet.
When you feel the sting of power used to oppress rather than
serve, let it spur you to humility in how you exercise power.

1 John 1:5—2:2
Psalm 124:2–3,4–5,7b–8
Matthew 2:13–18

Whoever hates his brother is in darkness;
he walks in darkness
and does not know where he is going
because the darkness has blinded his eyes.
—1 JOHN 2:11

We live in contentious times. Individuals and groups spend a lot of time and energy spreading suspicion and fear and demonizing other people and groups. Categorizing people as "other" in our mind can easily turn into hate of our brothers and sisters, and, as John the Evangelist warns, hate will blind us. Most of us would say that we stop well short of hate. We will admit to getting justifiably angry and cling to negative thinking. The point is, the world desperately needs more love. It's the only thing that can heal the divisions. Jesus tells us to quit sorting people into us versus them and instead love one another as he has loved us.

1 John 2:3–11
Psalm 96:1–2a,2b–3,5b–6
Luke 2:22–35

Put on, as God's chosen ones, holy and beloved,
heartfelt compassion, kindness, humility, gentleness,
and patience,
bearing with one another and forgiving one another.
—COLOSSIANS 3:12–13

St. Paul offers an excellent recipe for how we can all get along. Perhaps the most underappreciated virtue in his list is "bearing with one another." Whether with family members, coworkers, or people in the next pew, some people are bound to have quirks and foibles that get under our skin, causing distance where solidarity belongs. And, God knows, we have our own irritating ways as well. It takes a decision to not only overlook but to bear with such irritations. Today, practice seeing the presence of Christ in others, especially those who quickly get on your last nerve.

Sirach 3:2–6,12–14 or Colossians 3:12–21 or 3:12–17
Psalm 128:1–2,3,4–5
Matthew 2:13–15,19–23

Saturday

DECEMBER 31

• ST. SYLVESTER I, POPE •

What came to be through him was life,
and this life was the light of the human race;
the light shines in the darkness,
and the darkness has not overcome it.
—JOHN 1:3–5

When I was a kid, right around this time of year the electricity went out in our neighborhood. It was a cold, dark night, and I was frightened. And then a wondrous thing happened. Little by little, candlelight flickered in the houses and two-flats up and down our street. In our house, too, Mom dug out the candles and placed them around the room.

We all have a light inside us, our share of the spark of creation. That night, people let their lights shine, and the darkness did not overcome it. Happy New Year! May your light shine bright in the coming year.

1 John 2:18–21
Psalm 96:1–2,11–12,13
John 1:1–18

JANUARY 1

• THE SOLEMNITY OF MARY, THE HOLY MOTHER OF GOD •

And Mary kept all these things,
reflecting on them in her heart.
—LUKE 2:19

Mary was a ponderer. She kept the reality of all that
happened to her in her heart and pondered it. Pondering is
not the same as "thinking things through" or "making up my
mind." It's an act of faith, faith that there is more to the world
than meets the physical eye. Pondering is having the
confidence that the Holy Spirit acts in the world—including
my world. Some see faith as achieving a level of certainty,
but pondering leads us elsewhere. It leads to revelation,
where we slowly come to see as Jesus sees and love as Jesus
loves. As we begin a new year, I invite you to join me in
making 2023 a year of pondering all that God is doing in
our lives.

Numbers 6:22–27
Psalm 67:2–3,5,6,8 (2a)
Galatians 4:4–7
Luke 2:16–21

• ST. BASIL THE GREAT AND ST. GREGORY NAZIANZEN, BISHOPS AND
DOCTORS OF THE CHURCH •

"I am the voice of one crying out in the desert,
'Make straight the way of the Lord.'"
—JOHN 1:23

How would it go if you ran into John the Baptist and he urged you to repent? Some who heard him eagerly embraced his message and changed their hearts. Others were so offended they had him put to death. It's uncomfortable to be judged, but judgment is an essential part of spiritual growth. If judgment comes across as condemnation, it's nearly impossible to receive it well. But John preached a call to change based on hope—the hope that however painful changing my ways might be, the result will be freedom and a restoration to wholeness. God, when I hear a call to change and it gets my back up, grant me a hopeful heart so I can welcome the grace of that moment.

1 John 2:22–28
Psalm 98:1,2–3ab,3cd–4
John 1:19–28

JANUARY 3

Behold, the Lamb of God.
—JOHN 1:33

What does it mean to "behold" something or someone? To behold is akin to pondering. It is an act of wonder rather than judgment. Wonder requires being open to mystery, something our critical minds aren't inclined to do. Acting out of the critical mind, we are quick to evaluate, compare, and make snap judgments based on an outer view. When we behold, we allow the true, deeper reality of a person to reveal itself to us. It's how deep friendships happen. And it's also how the awakening of our most precious self—the one created in the image and likeness of God—begins. Today, behold the Lamb of God in the many ways Jesus appears to you in your coworkers, your family members, the stranger on the street.

1 John 2:29—3:6
Psalm 98:1,3cd–4,5–6
John 1:29–34

JANUARY 4

Jesus turned and saw them following him
and said to them,
"What are you looking for?"
—1 JOHN 1:36

Imagine yourself in today's Gospel story. Crowds have gathered around Jesus. John the Baptist points him out for you, and you move to follow him—from a distance. Jesus notices you following him and asks, "What are you looking for?" If it were me, my first temptation would be to blather on with flattery, quoting some of his best lines to him, and weaving in some facts about me that would make me look good. But he'd see right through all that, ask the question again, and turn to walk on, leaving the question where it belonged: with me. Ego always speaks first in situations like this. Better that I should be still, behold the man, and ponder the question.

1 John 3:7–10
Psalm 98:1,7–8,9
John 1:35–42

Thursday

JANUARY 5

• ST. JOHN NEUMANN, BISHOP •

But Nathanael said to him,
"Can anything good come from Nazareth?"
Philip said to him, "Come and see."
—JOHN 1:46

Jesus is on the move, and if you want to know what Jesus
knows and see what Jesus sees, you'll need to get up and
follow. In yesterday's Gospel, Peter and Philip ask Jesus
where he is staying, and he answers, "Come, and you will
see." Today, Nathaniel wonders whether anything good can
come from Nazareth, Jesus' hometown. This time Philip says,
"Come and see." In these two passages we have a clarifying
glimpse of how faith is entered and how disciples are made.
Both the how and the why of faith flow from following Jesus.
We'll never comprehend them if we stand at a distance
and judge.

1 John 3:11–21
Psalm 100:1b–2,3,4,5
John 1:43–51

I have baptized you with water;
he will baptize you with the Holy Spirit.
—MARK 1:8

How should we approach Gospel stories? Theologian and Scripture scholar John Shea offers a helpful perspective: "Jesus is not a straightforward conveyor of information. He is an encounter with higher consciousness that is bent on opening whomever he meets to the indwelling of Spirit." The key word for me is *encounter*. Jesus meets us where we are, with the intention of opening our eyes and minds to the presence of Spirit within. When we approach each Gospel passage as an encounter with Jesus, the experience gains an immediacy we won't know if we view the Gospels simply as that which happened long ago.

1 John 5:5–13
Psalm 147:12–13,14–15,19–20
Mark 1:7–11 or Luke 3:23–38 or 3:23,31–34,36,38

JANUARY 7

*Jesus did this as the beginning of his signs
at Cana in Galilee,
and so revealed his glory.*
—JOHN 2:11

It came to 750 gallons. That's how much water Jesus turned into wine to re-enliven the wedding feast at Cana. It was the first sign, the first miracle of his public life. So either, being a novice, he made a mistake or, being Jesus, he was making a point. The point he was making was that his arrival on the scene unleashes a superabundant outpouring of spirit. Not just a little bit over the norm, but in an amount that people would be talking about two thousand-plus years later. This was the first clue at what God had in store for us by sending his son. We'll see soon enough that he's holding nothing back.

1 John 5:14–21
Psalm 149:1–2,3–4,5 and 6a and 9b
John 2:1–11

Sunday

JANUARY 8

• THE EPIPHANY OF THE LORD •

*And having been warned in a dream not to return
to Herod,
they departed for their country by another way.*
—MATTHEW 2:12

The story of the Magi has all the plot elements of a
blockbuster thriller. In a far-off land, wise seekers learn that a
messiah is about to be born. On their journey to pay
homage, they encounter (cue the menacing music!)
self-seeking leaders dedicated to protecting their power at all
costs. There, the travelers receive both helpful advice and
troubling instructions. Confused but determined, they
continue to follow their star. Arriving at their destination,
they discover a markedly different scene than the halls of
power they recently left: a place of simplicity, tenderness,
inclusion, and love. Thus, hope and fear are set against each
other. Which side will win? Whom shall we trust?

Isaiah 60:1–6
Psalm 72:1–2,7–8,10–11,12–13
Ephesians 3:2–3a,5–6
Matthew 2:1–12

*"This is my beloved son with whom I am
well pleased."*
—MATTHEW 3:17

Baptism is a sacrament rich in symbol and ripe with meaning.
The water brings cleansing from the stain of sin, both our
personal sins and the effects of original sin. Being plunged
into the water and rising up again is a symbol of dying to an
old life and rising up anew. It's a foretaste of both Jesus' death
and our own. In the outpouring of the Holy Spirit, baptism
also reveals our true identity as a beloved daughter or son of
God. The words Jesus heard from the Father echo the words
culminating in creation: "And God said, 'It is very good.' "
Baptism reveals that we live in a benign world where we are
worthy and God is for us, a sacred mystery worth
pondering today.

Isaiah 42:1–4,6–7 or Acts 10:34–38
Psalm 29:1–2,3–4,3,9–10 (11b)
Matthew 3:13–17

Tuesday

JANUARY 10

*In their synagogue was a man with an unclean spirit;
he cried out, "What have you to do with us,
Jesus of Nazareth?"*
—MARK 1:23–24

The unclean spirit cried out, "What have you to do with us, Jesus of Nazareth?" Jesus' actions revealed, "I have everything to do with you. I have come to free people from your harm." Unclean spirits of all sorts prefer to stay hidden. They don't like to be noticed. I don't want anyone—least of all myself—to see that sometimes my sharing stories with others is really gossip meant to make me feel superior. And my rushing to help others is sometimes an attempt to make myself look good. Demons of all shapes and strengths need to be brought into the light of day. Jesus can help. That's why he came.

Hebrews 2:5–12
Psalm 8:2ab and 5,6–7,8–9
Mark 1:21–28
Or Hebrews 1:1–6 and 2:5–12 / Mark 1:14–20 and 1:21–28

JANUARY 11

Rising very early before dawn,
he left and went off to a deserted place,
where he prayed.
—MARK 1:35

I tried rising before dawn to go to a deserted place in the house and pray. I hit the snooze alarm or plowed into working instead. So I made a list of ways to add more prayer to my day. Here are some that worked: pray when someone cuts me off in traffic, whenever I hear an ambulance siren, when an old friend comes to mind, when I feel the grip of fear around my heart, before a meeting that makes me anxious, or after a meeting that has left me hurt or angry, before every meal—even the ones eaten in the car out of a paper bag, before returning home at the end of the day. Start your own list. It works wonders.

Hebrews 2:14–18
Psalm 105:1–2,3–4,6–7,8–9
Mark 1:29–39

JANUARY 12

The Holy Spirit says:
Oh, that today you would hear his voice,
"Harden not your hearts."
—HEBREWS 3:7–8

Spiritually speaking, there are few things more difficult to
overcome than a hardened heart. The Holy Spirit does
wonders when invited and is always at work behind the
scenes. But the Holy Spirit won't override a hardened heart.
"I just can't let go," we say. "I'll never forgive her/him." "I'm
too ashamed of what I've done." "I'll surrender everything but
that!" We grow attached to our wound, our guilt, our hurt,
our shame. It becomes a strange god we've given our power
over to. If even the tiniest corner of your heart is hardened,
simply pray daily, "Loving God, help me loosen my grip on
whatever it is that keeps me from you. Give me a heart of
flesh."

Hebrews 3:7–14
Psalm 95:6–7c,8–9,10–11
Mark 1:40–45

JANUARY 13

• ST. HILARY, BISHOP AND DOCTOR OF THE CHURCH •

Unable to get near Jesus because of the crowd,
they opened up the roof above him.
After they had broken through,
they let down the mat on which the paralytic
was lying.
When Jesus saw their faith, he said to him,
"Child, your sins are forgiven."
—MARK 2:3–5

The Gospel says, "When Jesus saw their faith," he was moved to action. What did Jesus see? He saw compassion in action. He saw the love of friends played out for all to see. The once-paralyzed man walked out that day a healed and forgiven man. Yet the griping scribes looking on saw none of that. When miracles happen, what do I see? The faith of others? God's power at work? Or distress that things didn't transpire the way I expected?

Hebrews 4:1–5,11
Psalm 78:3 and 4bc,6c–7,8
Mark 2:1–12

JANUARY 14

Let the words of my mouth and the thought of my heart
find favor before you,
O LORD, my rock and my redeemer
—PSALM 19:15

I recently saw a poster saying, "Words are free. It's how you use them that may cost you." I cringe when I recall times when a thoughtless word I spoke hurt a friend or bruised a coworker. And I wonder how my self-seeking speech has disappointed God. Usually, my words go astray when I'm experiencing unacknowledged fear, anger, or resentment. Today, before opening my mouth, I will be mindful of my emotional state and ask God's help in speaking from a place of compassion and grace.

Hebrews 4:12–16
Psalm 19:8,9,10,15
Mark 2:13–17

JANUARY 15

I will make you a light to the nations,
that my salvation may reach to the ends of the earth.
—ISAIAH 49:6

I'm a big fan of good eulogies. I love it when, at a memorial service or funeral, a family member or longtime friend recounts the ways the good news of Jesus can be detected in the life and actions of the dear departed. It's inspiring to hear how the deceased has been a light to others during their lives, often in quite ordinary and unselfconscious ways. Through random acts of kindness, generosity, moral courage, or fidelity, the one who has passed has helped salvation reach to the ends of the earth. Today, ask God to let the light of Christ shine through you to those you will encounter.

Isaiah 49:3,5–6
Psalm 40:2,4,7–8,8–9,10 (8a,9a)
1 Corinthians 1:1–3
John 1:29–34

Son though he was, he learned obedience
from what he suffered.
—HEBREWS 5:8

Obedience is a frequently underestimated virtue because it's so easily misunderstood. Many see it as blindly giving over one's will to the authority of another. Fr. Ronald Rolheiser sees it more as "a radical submitting of one's human ego (with all its wounds, desires, lusts, private ambitions, and envies) to something and Someone higher than oneself." Obedience helps us move beyond a childish pursuit of "freedom from" all constraints and move to attain "freedom for" selfless love and service. True obedience gives us the freedom to step into our life without inner conflict and resistance, and freedom to embrace our purpose and calling. Ponder Jesus brought before Pilate, beaten, shackled. And yet his radical obedience enables him to stand there totally free.

Hebrews 5:1–10
Psalm 110:1,2,3,4
Mark 2:18–22

JANUARY 17

• ST. ANTHONY, ABBOT •

This we have as an anchor of the soul,
sure and firm, which reaches into the interior
behind the veil,
where Jesus has entered on our behalf.
—HEBREWS 6:19–20

The "anchor of the soul" that Paul talks about is God's promise to Abraham: "I will bless you and multiply you." In essence, God is saying, "I will take care of you and your family, generation after generation." God reveals that creation is benign and that he is *for* us. What a calming anchor for the soul, a promise to rely on amid constant change in every aspect of human life. When you are feeling distressed, cling to the anchor that can steady your boat even in stormy seas.

Hebrews 6:10–20
Psalm 111:1–2,4–5,9 and 10c
Mark 2:23–28

There was a man there who had a withered hand.
They watched Jesus closely
to see if he would cure him on the sabbath
so that they might accuse him.
—MARK 3:1–2

Has someone watched you like a hawk, hoping to catch you
goofing up? Jesus got that a lot. We can learn from him how
best to deal with such situations. Look to your mission.
Notice how Jesus responded, in this case asking, "Is it lawful
to do good on the sabbath rather than to do evil?" He was
calling his critics to see the greater good he was seeking.
Jesus was focused on healing and making whole. When Jesus
gazed upon individuals, he looked to see how he might bring
abundant life. His critics didn't see people, only infractions.

Hebrews 7:1–3,15–17
Psalm 110:1,2,3,4
Mark 3:1–6

Thursday

JANUARY 19

Hearing what he was doing,
a large number of people came to him also
from Jerusalem,
from Idumea, from beyond the Jordan.
—MARK 3:8

People heard that Jesus was healing people and casting out demons. They travelled great distances to see him. Some even came "from beyond the Jordan," which brings to mind not only Jesus' baptism in the Jordan but also my own baptism. Sometimes, through busyness or lack of perseverance, I figuratively wander off "beyond the Jordan." I lose sight of who I am and what I believe in. And then I hear or see something that reminds me that I am a beloved child of God; I return to that closeness with Jesus where my soul can be healed and my inner demons silenced. Listen for that Word calling you back today to where you once belonged.

Hebrews 7:25—8:6
Psalm 40:7–8a,8b–9,10,17
Mark 3:7–12

JANUARY 20

• ST. FABIAN, POPE AND MARTYR * ST. SEBASTIAN, MARTYR •

I will put my laws in their minds
and I will write them upon their hearts.
—HEBREWS 8:10

Once, on a pilgrimage, our group stayed overnight at the
mountaintop abbey at Montserrat, in Spain. Someone
suggested we all rise before dawn, walk out to a promontory,
and witness what turned out to be the most awe-inspiring
sunrise any of us had experienced. At the wrap-up meeting
on the last night of the pilgrimage, almost everyone
mentioned that sunrise experience as the one in which they
most experienced the presence of God. Many said their faith
was greatly deepened; others said their troubling doubts had
subsided as the dawn from on high broke upon us. With
loving care for each of us, God had once again written on
our hearts. Recall and ponder a sacred experience you've had.

Hebrews 8:6–13
Psalm 85:8 and 10,11–12,13–14
Mark 3:13–19

———————————

JANUARY 21

He entered once for all into the sanctuary,
not with the blood of goats and calves
but with his own Blood,
thus obtaining eternal redemption.
—HEBREWS 9:12

There is mystery and power in blood. We sense it innately. When someone sheds their blood for God and others, we call it the ultimate sacrifice, and we are hushed. Words cannot adequately convey its meaning, and they needn't. I came across a quote, often attributed to Joyce Carol Oates: "We are linked by blood, and blood is memory without language." So when Jesus held the cup, blessed it, and offered it, saying, "Do this in memory of me," he was offering a kind of blood transfusion, replacing memory of original sin with the memory of all that he said and did during his earthly life. Next time you receive the Eucharist, be aware of all that is being offered to you.

Hebrews 9:2–3,11–14
Psalm 47:2–3,6–7,8–9
Mark 3:20–21

JANUARY 22

When Jesus heard that John had been arrested,
he withdrew to Galilee.
—MATTHEW 4:12

The word *withdrew* sounds as if Jesus is backing away out of
fear of Herod, but in fact, he strides confidently to Galilee,
where Herod ruled. What's more, we learn that "he went all
around Galilee," teaching, proclaiming the Good News, and
healing all who were suffering. He was not hiding his light.
But neither was he taunting Herod. He had a mission, and he
went about it with all he had, even gathering disciples to
work alongside him. Fear is powerful, and there are few
things stronger than fear. One is embracing your mission and
pouring your heart, body, mind, and soul into it. If fear is
keeping you from stepping boldly into life today, ask Jesus
for the gifts of courage and zeal.

Isaiah 8:23—9:3
Psalm 27:1,4,13–14 (1a)
1 Corinthians 1:10–13,17
Matthew 4:12–23 or 4:12–17

Monday

JANUARY 23

And if a house is divided against itself,
that house will not be able to stand.
—MARK 3:25

A good friend of mine, a recovering addict, talks about his
life before recovery as a "house divided." "What started as
secrets became lies, and eventually I crossed one moral
boundary after another," he told me. "I was spiritually
bankrupt when I came across a quote from Dr. Thomas Hora:
'All problems are psychological, but all solutions are
spiritual.'"[1] Sin is divisive. It pits us not only against God but
also against ourselves. The pain of this dissonance drives us
to secrecy and more sin, creating a widening rift in our
psyche for which we pay an enormous price. My friend says,
"Every morning, I invite Jesus, the great healer, into my life
to restore me to integrity."

Hebrews 9:15,24–28
Psalm 98:1,2–3ab,3cd–4,5–6
Mark 3:22–30

1. Thomas Hora, MD, *Beyond the Dream: Awakening to Reality* (New York: Crossroad Publishing,
1996), 130.

Tuesday

JANUARY 24

The mother of Jesus and his brothers arrived
at the house.
Standing outside, they sent word to Jesus and called him.
—MARK 3:31

Catholics have been taught that Jesus experienced everything we do except sin. In today's reading, he experienced a very common challenge: misunderstandings in the family. Put yourself in the scene: Jesus' cousin John had been arrested and would soon be killed. Scribes and Pharisees were stalking Jesus, hoping to catch him uttering blasphemy. Jesus' growing popularity was threatening religious and political leaders. And so his extended family members showed up where he was preaching out of concern for his safety. Though Jesus and his family clearly loved one another, I can imagine that this might have been a standoff that would take time to settle. Sound familiar?

Hebrews 10:1–10
Psalm 40:2 and 4ab,7–8a,10,11
Mark 3:31–35

⇒ 59 ⇐

$\mathcal{W}ednesday$

JANUARY 25

• THE CONVERSION OF ST. PAUL THE APOSTLE •

"I fell to the ground and heard a voice saying to me,
"Saul, Saul, why are you persecuting me?"
I replied, 'Who are you, sir?'
And he said to me,
'I am Jesus the Nazorean whom you are persecuting.'"
—ACTS 22:7–8

Saul's account of coming to faith in Jesus has inspired
countless conversions. On his way to Damascus a great light
shone around him and he heard a voice: "Why are you
persecuting me?" Saul asked, "Who are you?" Paul learned in
this dramatic encounter that faith is not obeying a list of
rules, which he had obsessively been trying to do. Faith is a
relationship, a response to God's invitation to see our lives as
they are and as they might become. Ponder the elements of
St. Paul's conversion. Let them inspire you to a deeper
relationship with Jesus.

Acts 22:3–16 or 9:1–22
Psalm 117:1bc,2
Mark 16:15–18

⋟ 60 ⋞

JANUARY 26

[Jesus said,] "Take care what you hear."
—MARK 4:24

Years ago I had a summer job involving tedious work. I looked forward to eating lunch with a trio of very funny people. They were also caustic, turning their weapons of wit toward every target imaginable: management, celebrities, coworkers, and surely me when I wasn't around. After a few days, I was not only taking in their demeaning talk but also contributing my own. Lunch left me with a sour attitude and an unquiet soul. I decided to eat lunch on the loading dock, where the air was fresh. Each day I'd be visited by the dock manager, a soft-spoken man whose heart was full of kindness for all. The work was still tedious, but after talking with the dock chief, my heart was replenished with easygoing joy.

Take care what you hear.

2 Timothy 1:1–8 or Titus 1:1–5
Psalm 96:1–2a,2b–3,7–8a,10
Mark 4:21–25

• ST. ANGELA MERICI, VIRGIN •

*"This is how it is with the Kingdom of God;
it is as if a man were to scatter seed on the land
and would sleep and rise night and day
and the seed would sprout and grow,
he knows not how."*
—MARK 4:26–27

People want to know outcomes ahead of time. It's human nature. But Jesus tells us that in the kingdom of God things happen in their own way and on their own schedule. We "know not how." We can't alter outcomes by our wanting or worrying. It seems that the worst outcome is for people to lose confidence in God and the future and take no positive action for fear of what might or might not happen. Faith prompts us to keep taking action and keep planting seeds, knowing that God is at work in all of his creation—even in us.

Hebrews 10:32–39
Psalm 37:3–4,5–6,23–24,39–40
Mark 4:26–34

> *He woke up,*
> *rebuked the wind,*
> *and said to the sea, "Quiet! Be still!"*
> *The wind ceased and there was great calm.*
> *Then he asked them, "Why are you terrified?*
> *Do you not yet have faith?"*
> —MARK 4:39–40

Fear and faith. These two foes face off against each other repeatedly in the New Testament. I've heard it said that fear and faith cannot exist in one heart at the same time. I'm not so sure it's as cut and dried as that. But I do know that the remedy for my crippling fear is faith, and not as some "get out of jail free" card I can simply wave around to make the fear vanish. Faith is not magic; it's opening our heart to a relationship of trust with the living God. Trust in God, and let your heart be calm.

Hebrews 11:1–2,8–19
Luke 1:69–70,71–72,73–75
Mark 4:35–41

JANUARY 29

• FOURTH SUNDAY IN ORDINARY TIME •

When Jesus saw the crowds, he went up the mountain,
and after he had sat down, his disciples came to him.
He began to teach, saying:
"Blessed are the poor in spirit."
—MATTHEW 5:1–3

The Beatitudes could be called "How God Sees Things."
Jesus gathered the disciples close around him so they could
learn to see how he and the Father see. The Beatitudes reveal
what it would take for peace and justice to reign. They don't
overlook the negative circumstances of life, but neither do
they ignore the blessedness that is available in those very
circumstances to help us bring life in line with God's will.
They acknowledge the difficult truth that blessedness incites
evil responses. Resisting that evil is its own act of
blessedness, which will not be overcome. Blessed are you.

Zephaniah 2:3; 3:12–13
Psalm 146:6–7,8–9,9–10
1 Corinthians 1:26–31
Matthew 5:1–12a

JANUARY 30

When he got out of the boat,
at once a man from the tombs
who had an unclean spirit met him.
The man had been dwelling among the tombs,
and no one could restrain him any longer,
even with a chain.
—MARK 5:2–3

I can relate to this man so tormented by demons that he chose to live among the tombs. At times, I abandon life-giving practices, and I isolate, cutting myself off from sources of life. I wallow in harmful habits and negative thinking. At worst, I lose trust that Jesus can set me free. When that happens, I've learned to put myself in the way of grace. I increase my prayer time, get to Mass, hang around for fellowship, do something helpful for another. Through these encounters with Christ, I abandon the tombs and find my way home.

Hebrews 11:32–40
Psalm 31:20,21,22,23,24
Mark 5:1–20

JANUARY 31

• ST. JOHN BOSCO, PRIEST •

Since we are surrounded by so great a cloud of witnesses,
let us rid ourselves of every burden and sin
that clings to us
and persevere in running the race that lies before us.
—HEBREWS 12:1

Everybody needs a crew, those who surround you and
support the best in you. I recently took my
ninety-four-year-old mother to the cemetery. She had been
feeling unmoored with the recent loss of longtime family and
friends. We visited the family plot, walking through the rows
of people with whom we had celebrated so many holidays,
first communions, weddings, funerals, and ordinary life. We
told stories at each gravestone, taking to heart the testimony
of the lives of those we came to visit. We drove away,
strengthened for the race that lies before us.

Hebrews 12:1–4
Psalm 22:26b–27,28 and 30,31–32
Mark 5:21–43

FEBRUARY 1

*Make straight paths for your feet,
that what is lame may not be dislocated but healed.*
—HEBREWS 12:13

There's an old joke about a guy who rushes into a doctor's office flapping his arms like a chicken and saying, "Doc, Doc, it hurts when I do this!" Mimicking the man's flapping, the doctor retorts, "Well, stop doing this!" I can find myself having that same inner conversation during my own daily *examen*. I recognize a pattern of feeling anger, sadness, or guilt because I keep tripping over the same moral stumbling blocks. I want God to cure the pain of stumbling rather than help me see how to remove the stumbling block. What could I, with God's help, remove from my path today (a habit, a Web site, gossiping with a toxic "friend") so that I can move toward holiness rather than stumble yet again?

Hebrews 12:4–7,11–15
Psalm 103:1–2,13–14,17–18a
Mark 6:1–6

FEBRUARY 2

Lift up, O gates, your lintels
reach up, you ancient portals,
that the king of glory may come in!
—PSALM 24:7

There are days when I barely lift my head at all. I might as
well have been on a conveyor belt all day, being carried
along, totally unaware of what's going on around me. Today,
I was shoveling snow, and I was going about it like a robot:
shovel, step, shovel, step, shovel, step. At one point I
stopped for a breather and looked up at the sky. Huge
snowflakes were tumbling down, falling like grace.
Neighbors waved; kids were making snow people. Across the
street I saw the half-dome apse of our parish church
blanketed in white. I was finally seeing. Before that moment
of pausing, the King of glory could have walked right by, and
I would never have known.

Malachi 3:1–4
Psalm 24:7,8,9,10
Heb 2:14–18
Luke 2:22–40 or 22:22–32

Remember your leaders who spoke the word
of God to you.
Consider the outcome of their way of life
and imitate their faith.
—HEBREWS 13:7

When I gave talks to parents about passing on a living faith, I would start by asking them to think about an adult from their youth who had a positive influence on their faith. I'd invite them to consider who it was, what key lesson they conveyed, and how that message was delivered. It was often quite a moving time, and people were eager to tell others in their small group about the person who helped introduce them to a life of faith. Who fanned the spark of faith in your early life? Spend time pondering how the ripples of goodness they're responsible for continue to flow through you and others.

Hebrews 13:1–8
Psalm 27:1,3,5,8b–9abc
Mark 6:14–29

Saturday

FEBRUARY 4

When Jesus disembarked and saw the vast crowd,
his heart was moved with pity for them,
for they were like sheep without a shepherd;
and he began to teach them many things.
—MARK 6:34

When we have had an experience of the Spirit, we will want to
share it. Steeped in the Spirit, Jesus' desire to share what he
experienced energized his public life. When he "saw" the vast
crowd, he didn't just see them with the eye of the flesh. He saw
them also with the eye of the soul. They longed for God,
mercy, and justice but didn't know how to attain them. They
believed Jesus could show them the way. In time, they
discovered he *is* the Way. You have had an experience of the
Spirit. People look to you to be shown the way. Do you
see them?

Hebrews 13:15–17,20–21
Psalm 23:1–3a,3b–4,5,6
Mark 6:30–34

Sunday

FEBRUARY 5

• FIFTH SUNDAY IN ORDINARY TIME •

"You are the light of the world. . . .
Just so, your light must shine before others
that they may see your good deeds,
and glorify your heavenly Father."
—MATTHEW 5:14,16

The committee that meets inside my head was called to order as the Gospel was about to be proclaimed. Worrier wondered if someone left the stove on. Procrastinator anxiously recognized he's running out of weekend. Sir Ego was judging others around him. And Still, Small Voice waited patiently for a word of life. "You are the Light of the World," proclaimed the deacon. "What now?" asked Worrier. "Your light must shine before others." "Who's got time for that?" griped Procrastinator. "That they may see your good deeds."

"Now we're talking!" grinned Sir Ego. "And glorify your heavenly Father." "Ah, yes! Now I see," said Still, Small Voice.

Isaiah 58:7–10
Psalm 112:4–5,6–7,8–9 (4a)
1 Corinthians 2:1–5
Matthew 5:13–16

FEBRUARY 6

You send forth springs into the watercourses
that wind among the mountains.
Beside them the birds of heaven dwell,
from among the branches they send forth their song.
—PSALM 104:10 AND 12

It's a cold, dark day as I write this reflection. Yet the phrase "from among the branches they send forth their song" transports me to another place and time. It's early summer, and dawn is breaking at my brother's cottage on a lovely spring-fed Michigan lake. My kayak glides softly beneath low-hanging branches along the far, undeveloped shore. Birds send forth their songs. I cease paddling and am bathed in dappled sunlight and birdsong. Creation is the first Gospel, revealing God's glory, majesty, and generative love. Listen!

Genesis 1:1–19
Psalm 104:1–2a,5–6,10 and 12,24 and 35c
Mark 6:53–56

FEBRUARY 7

Then God said:
"Let us make man in our image, after our likeness."
—GENESIS 1:26

I find it fascinating that when someone is arrogant and brash and bosses people around, others might say, "He thinks he's God." Is that really who we think God is—a tinhorn bully? We are made in the image and likeness of God. What does that say about us? That means humans are capable of understanding, in part at least, God's plan and desire for the world. And that makes us cocreators with God. God's image is indelible. As for the likeness, I suspect that's something we have to grow into as we grow in holiness.

Genesis 1:20—2:4a
Psalm 8:4–5,6–7,8–9
Mark 7:1–13

FEBRUARY 8

• ST. JEROME EMILIANI, PRIEST • ST. JOSEPHINE BAKHITA, VIRGIN •

But a stream was welling up out of the earth
and was watering all the surface of the ground—
the LORD God formed man out of the clay
of the ground
and blew into his nostrils the breath of life.
—GENESIS 2:6–7

In today's reading from Genesis, we're told of a stream, a symbol of the Holy Spirit, welling up out of the earth. In Revelation, the last book of the Bible, we are told of "the river of life that flows from the throne of God." From the beginning of the story of our salvation to its final chapter, God has poured out divine life for us at every turn. Whenever you see water, ponder the ways God's grace continues to flow into and shape your life.

Genesis 2:4b–9,15–17
Psalm 104:1–2a,27–28,29bc–30
Mark 7:14–23

FEBRUARY 9

*That is why a man leaves his father and mother
and clings to his wife,
and the two of them become one flesh.*
—GENESIS 2:24

Here's a joke I would tell when talking to married couples.
"When a couple gets married, the two shall become one. And
the only question is, which one?" It always got a laugh
because couples know that achieving marital unity is tough.
And then they'd turn and smile at one another, because
couples know that achieving that unity is well worth any
struggle. The idea that God took a rib from Adam and
fashioned Eve from it may seem ridiculous. But I find the
story a compelling response to the question, "Why does my
eighty-two-year-old friend smile each day as he goes to visit
his 'sweetie,' his wife of sixty years who no longer recognizes
his face?"

Genesis 2:18–25
Psalm 128:1–2,3,4–5
Mark 7:24–30

• ST. SCHOLASTICA, VIRGIN •

Then I acknowledged my sin to you,
my guilt I covered not.
I said, "I confess my faults to the LORD,"
and you took away the guilt of my sin.
—PSALM 32:5

A woman shared this brief conversation between her and her college-age son. "Ma, I'm not going to confession anymore. Why are you harassing me about this?" His mother sighed and said, "You're old enough. I can't make you go. But if I stopped going, I'd have one question for myself: How am I planning to handle my guilt?" In my experience, there are some sins, some betrayals of ourselves or others, that only God can forgive. They need to be acknowledged. Hiding our guilt will not eliminate its impact. It will fester and make our lives smaller. We are not our own saviors.

Genesis 3:1–8
Psalm 32:1–2,5,6,7
Mark 7:31–37

Saturday

FEBRUARY 11

• OUR LADY OF LOURDES •

Teach us to number our days aright,
that we may gain wisdom of heart.
—PSALM 90:12

St. Ignatius of Loyola considered the daily *examen* to be one of the most powerful spiritual practices for strengthening our faith. This simple five-step exercise can be done anywhere, anytime, and takes less than fifteen minutes. Here's how it works: (1) Get quiet and ask God for light to see yourself clearly. (2) Be grateful. Give thanks to God for gifts received. (3) Review the past twenty-four hours, guided by the Holy Spirit. Notice when you were closer to or farther away from God. (4) Face your shortcomings in light of God's mercy. (5) Look toward the day to come with hope. Make this a daily practice, and you'll come to see how God is at work in your life.

Genesis 3:9–24
Psalm 90:2,3–4abc,5–6,12–13
Mark 8:1–10

⇒ 77 ⇐

FEBRUARY 12

"You have heard that it was said to your ancestors,
You shall not kill; and whoever kills
will be liable to judgment.
But I say to you,
whoever is angry with his brother
will be liable to judgment."
—MATTHEW 5:21–22

Thus begins a series of almost shocking declarations by Jesus about anger, lust, resentment, and lies. They are crafted to jolt us into a reflective awareness of the inner states that drive our outer behavior. Murder may be the outcome, but such sins begin in the hidden harbors of our hearts. The more we acknowledge those inner stirrings and bring them into the light of his love, the sooner we will be free of the need to enact them. Every gardener knows you need to expose the roots of weeds if you really want the weeds to disappear.

Sirach 15:15–20
Psalm 119:1–2,4–5,17–18,33–34 (1b)
1 Corinthians 2:6–10
Matthew 5:17–37 or 5:20–22a,27–28,33–34a,37

*Cain said to his brother Abel, "Let us go out
in the field."
When they were in the field,
Cain attacked his brother Abel and killed him.*
—GENESIS 4:8

The account of Cain and Abel is an ancient story that has been condensed over time, so some details are unclear. Like, what was wrong with Cain's offering? But one point comes through loud and clear: envy is powerful and has far-reaching impact. Yet it's so easy to succumb to this deadly sin. A coworker is praised in front of the group; a neighbor takes a winter trip to Hawaii; even a rival sports team's success—any of these can trigger reactions that poison the heart. As envy's poison grows, it feeds resentment and edges the one harboring it toward violence, whether passive-aggressive or full-strength aggressive-aggressive. One good antidote to envy, jealousy, and covetousness is making a gratitude list and harboring that in your heart instead.

Genesis 4:1–15,25
Psalm 50:1 and 8,16bc–17,20–21
Mark 8:11–13

FEBRUARY 14

• ST. CYRIL, MONK, AND ST. METHODIUS, BISHOP •

The voice of the LORD is over the waters. . . .
The God of glory thunders.
—PSALM 29:3,4

Sometimes life can feel chaotic, as if "the center will not hold." Today's reading, with its description of God's power, reminds me of the first moments of Genesis when "the earth was a formless wasteland, and darkness covered the abyss." One translation I read used *chaos* instead of *abyss*, and it dawned on me that God's initial act was to bring order out of chaos. In fact, chaos seems to be the medium in which God does his best work. The voice of God draws not only order but also light, life, meaning, and purpose out of chaos. I take comfort from the fact that he did it then and he can do it again in my life right now.

Genesis 6:5–8; 7:1–5,10
Psalm 29:1a and 2,3ac–4,3b and 9c–10
Mark 8:14–21

FEBRUARY 15

*Then he laid hands on the man's eyes
a second time and he saw clearly;
his sight was restored and he could see
everything distinctly.*
—MARK 8:25

When I look back through my old journals, I can see how
I've needed a second touch of grace from time to time. I find
passages where, with great excitement, I came to a new
insight or inner freedom, only to realize a short time later
that the work of grace was not finished with me in that area.

I frequently needed a second touch (or third or fourth
or . . .), often in the form of humility, for God's healing grace
to take effect. Grace works to perfect nature, and it does so
in its own time. My job is to trust that grace is at work in me
and to do nothing rash—like try to control the process—that
would get in God's way.

Genesis 8:6–13,20–22
Psalm 116:12–13,14–15,18–19
Mark 8:22–26

FEBRUARY 16

He asked his disciples,
"Who do people say that I am?"
They said in reply,
"John the Baptist, others Elijah,
still others one of the prophets."
And he asked them,
"But who do you say that I am?"
—MARK 8:27–29

Jesus uses a technique that teachers have used for centuries: introducing a topic with a universal question and then making it more specific to each of his hearers. He moved the question from the general (Who do people say I am?) to the personal (Who am I to *you*?). It was a move from speculation to commitment, from the head to the heart. Imagine yourself walking with Jesus and the disciples as he asked his second question. Dig deep. How would you respond?

Genesis 9:1–13
Psalm 102:16–18,19–21,29 and 22–23
Mark 8:27–33

Friday

FEBRUARY 17

• THE SEVEN HOLY FOUNDERS OF THE SERVITE ORDER •

*Jesus summoned the crowd with his disciples
and said to them,
"Whoever wishes to come after me must
deny himself
take up his cross, and follow me.
For whoever wishes to save his life will lose it,
but whoever loses his life for my sake
and that of the Gospel will save it."*
—MARK 8:34–35

It began with a summons. Jesus had something crucial to explain to those who wanted to follow him, and it's a paradox: if you want to save your life, you must lose it. The Gospels often seem to consist of endless accounts of Jesus trying to communicate how things work in the kingdom of God, while the disciples stay stuck in conventional wisdom. We get mired in conventional wisdom too. Next Wednesday, Lent begins, giving us a whole season to practice new ways of acting, which lead to new ways of being. Get ready.

Genesis 11:1–9
Psalm 33:10–11,12–13,14–15
Mark 8:34—9:1

FEBRUARY 18

*Faith is the realization of what is hoped for
and evidence of things not seen.*
—HEBREWS 11:1

Faith is a gift from God, a mystery we live our way into. Faith
is a relationship of trust that gives us the power to take the
next step when the path ahead is unknown. And faith
supplies the energy to stay the course when our initial
enthusiasm begins to wane. Faith is the voice inside telling us
that trying, and even failing, is worthwhile, if we are being
true to the One we have faith in. Faith not only changes
things around us but also changes us. It opens us up to all
God wants to do with us and for us. People often say, "Keep
the faith," but the truth is, faith keeps us.

Hebrews 11:1–7
Psalm 145:2–3,4–5,10–11
Mark 9:2–13

FEBRUARY 19

• SEVENTH SUNDAY IN ORDINARY TIME •

As far as the east is from the west,
so far has he put our transgressions from us.
—PSALM 103:12

Years ago, as a young editor at *U.S. Catholic* magazine, I was blustering one day about how people don't take sin seriously enough. A wonderful priest, Fr. James Maloney, CMF, talked to me after the meeting and gently said, "Tom, in all my years of hearing confessions I've come to understand that quite the opposite of what you said is true. In fact, what people don't take seriously enough is how eager God is to forgive their sins and free them from the burden of their guilt." That gave me a new way of thinking about people and sin, and I've witnessed that even those who claim not to believe in sin have a hard time letting go of guilt.

Leviticus 19:1–2,17–18
Psalm 103:1–2,3–4,8,10,12–13 (8a)
1 Corinthians 3:16–23
Matthew 5:38–48

Monday

FEBRUARY 20

*All wisdom comes from the LORD
and with him it remains forever.
The sands of the seashore, the drops of rain,
the days of eternity: who can number these?*
—SIRACH 1:1–2

Ah, wisdom! Who wouldn't want to be considered wise? The question is, how does one grow in wisdom? Sirach seems to think the path to wisdom begins with the jolt of humility we can feel at encountering the vastness of nature. "The sands of the seashore, the drops of rain," heaven's height, and earth's extent are realities only God comprehends; even thinking about them takes humans outside our ordinary realm where we feel in control. It requires a beginner's mind to become wise. A friend has a sign on his bulletin board at work: "Shut up and grow wise." Sir Francis Bacon put it a bit more eloquently: "Silence is the sleep that nourishes wisdom."

Sirach 1:1–10
Psalm 93:1ab,1cd–2,5
Mark 9:14–29

FEBRUARY 21

• ST. PETER DAMIAN, BISHOP AND DOCTOR OF THE CHURCH •

Trust God, and God will help you;
trust in him, and he will direct your way.
—SIRACH 2:6

In the midst of a very difficult time in my life, my spiritual director helped me recognize that though I had always believed in God, what I was struggling with was trusting God. Until then I hadn't seen the difference. I kept praying for God's help but wasn't prepared to accept that what was happening was indeed God's will. Sirach expresses great confidence in the trustworthiness of God and seems to suggest how we can grow in trust: exercise the virtue of hope, and don't wander from God's ways.

Sirach 2:1–11
Psalm 37:3–4,18–19,27–28,39–40
Mark 9:30–37

Even now, says the LORD,
return to me with your whole heart,
with fasting, and weeping, and mourning;
Rend your hearts, not your garments,
and return to the LORD, your God.
—JOEL 2:12–13

The beauty of the church year is that it makes room for every human reality, every mood, every existential question, every longing. Joel quickly sets the tone for Lent, and especially for Ash Wednesday, calling for fasting, weeping, and mourning.

In receiving the ashes, we have a powerful symbol that speaks universally in ways that words alone cannot convey. Watch the stream of people coming to be marked with ashes in the sign of the cross. Weak, strong, young, old, wealthy, impoverished, society's darlings, and society's overlooked, all come forward to be reminded of a truth that is so easy to forget: Remember, you are dust, and unto dust you shall return. Another point to ponder.

Joel 2:12–18
Psalm 51:3–4,5–6ab,12–13,14 and 17
2 Corinthians 5:20—6:2
Matthew 6:1–6,16–18

Blessed is the man who follows not
the counsel of the wicked,
Nor walks in the way of sinners,
nor sits in company of the insolent.
But delights in the law of the LORD
and meditates on this day and night.
—PSALM 1:1–2

Sister Daniel, OSB, a nun who taught me in grammar school, always urged us to "keep good companions." She knew that youngsters could be lured by others to do crazy and dangerous things they would never do on their own. Who are your daily companions at work, on your phone, in your earbuds, on TV, in the lunchroom? What messages are filling your mind and heart? How do you feel after spending time with each? What are you meditating on day and night? Would the wise Sister Daniel approve?

Deuteronomy 30:15–20
Psalm 1:1–2,3,4 and 6
Luke 9:22–25

This, rather, is the fasting that I wish:
releasing those bound unjustly,
untying the thongs of the yoke;
Setting free the oppressed,
breaking every yoke.
—ISAIAH 58:6

Fasting can be a tricky business. The ego can so quickly grab the limelight, and unintended hypocrisy can derail our efforts to grow closer to God. It doesn't pay to focus on that problem, however. That just keeps the focus on ourselves. Isaiah puts the focus on sharing our bread with the hungry and bringing the afflicted and the homeless into our house, or, at a minimum, into our consciousness. The fasting that God desires calls forth our integrity—doing the right things for the right reason. Forget yourself. Do for others.

Isaiah 58:1–9a
Psalm 51:3–4,5–6ab,18–19
Matthew 9:14–15

*The Pharisees and their scribes complained
to his disciples, saying,
"Why do you eat and drink with tax collectors
and sinners?"
Jesus said to them in reply,
"Those who are healthy do not need a physician,
but the sick do.
I have not come to call the righteous
to repentance but sinners."*
—LUKE 5:30–32

Thanks to the field of psychology, we have a word for it: *projection*. Truths that evoke shame in ourselves we project onto others. At the risk of projecting, I'll suggest that the Pharisees projected their own sense of sinfulness onto the tax collectors, an easy and obvious target. The thing is that Levi, the tax collector, admitted his own wrongdoings and chose to follow Jesus as the way out of his former life. The Pharisees couldn't acknowledge that; they were too busy judging others. Today, I pray that I may see others as Jesus sees them.

Isaiah 58:9b–14
Psalm 86:1–2,3–4,5–6
Luke 5:27–32

Sunday

FEBRUARY 26

• FIRST SUNDAY OF LENT •

But the gift is not like the transgression.
For if by that one person's transgression the many died,
how much more did the grace of God
and the gracious gift of the one man Jesus Christ
overflow for the many.
—ROMANS 5:15

It's hard to comprehend the reality of God's gift of mercy toward us. Conscientious believers can be far more aware of their sins than they are of God's forgiveness and compassion. St. Paul goes to great lengths to describe the magnitude of difference between our sin—the original sin of Adam and all subsequent sins perpetrated by the human race—and the pouring out of mercy by God, a grace that "overflow[s] for the many." At Mass we self-diagnose based on our fears, echoing the words of the centurion, "Lord, I am not worthy." In the Eucharist, Jesus offers a second opinion.

Genesis 2:7–9; 3:1–7
Psalm 51:3–4,5–6,12–13,17
Romans 5:12–19 or 5:12,17–19
Matthew 4:1–11

⇒ 92 ⇐

Monday

FEBRUARY 27

• ST. GREGORY OF NAREK, ABBOT AND DOCTOR OF THE CHURCH •

The LORD said to Moses,
"Speak to the whole assembly of the children
of Israel and tell them:
Be holy, for I, the LORD, your God, am holy."
—LEVITICUS 19:1–2

To be holy like God seems an impossible task. Fr. Ronald Rolheiser, OMI, describes two concepts of perfection. The Greek ideal is to have no deficiencies or flaws. In this concept, to be perfect is never to sin. In the Hebrew mindset, to be perfect is to walk with God, despite our flaws. Perfection here means "being in the divine presence" despite the fact that we are not perfect. The Greek version tends to hold sway in our culture, and it can be a useful motivating concept. But it's in the walking with God that we become holy. There are no self-made saints.

Leviticus 19:1–2,11–18
Psalm 19:8,9,10,15
Matthew 25:31–46

⇒ 93 ⇐

Tuesday

FEBRUARY 28

*So shall my word be
that goes forth from my mouth;
It shall not return to me void,
but shall do my will,
achieving the end for which I sent it.*
—ISAIAH 55:11

These lines from Isaiah describe the power of God's word, "achieving the end for which I sent it." The psalmist's previous lines reveal something important about the intention behind God's word and about the nature of its power. The psalm compares God's word to the falling rain that waters the earth, making it fertile and fruitful. And the psalm shows the end God has in mind: "giving seed to the one who sows and bread to the one who eats." Clearly God's word is for our benefit. It is sent forth to act within us to bring forth goodness and fruitfulness to us and to the world. Thanks be to God.

Isaiah 55:10–11
Psalm 34:4–5,6–7,16–17,18–19
Matthew 6:7–15

*"This generation is an evil generation;
it seeks a sign, but no sign will be given it,
except the sign of Jonah."*
—LUKE 11:29

Some who gathered around Jesus came seeking marvels on demand. But Jesus had a different agenda. He wanted more from them and more for them. He wanted all who came to receive the Word, but that wouldn't happen unless they had humble and contrite hearts. Which brings up Jonah, a prophet who arrogantly fled God's call to preach by hopping on a boat, only to end up spending three days in the belly of a large fish before being spit out where he began. Talk about humbling! Jonah's three days foreshadow the time Jesus spent in the tomb and point to our need to also experience the dying and the rising that are the Way of Jesus and the pattern of our salvation.

Jonah 3:1–10
Psalm 51:3–4,12–13,18–19
Luke 11:29–32

Thursday

MARCH 2

She lay prostrate upon the ground, together with her handmaids,
from morning until evening, and said:
"God of Abraham, God of Isaac, and God of Jacob, blessed are you.
Help me, who am alone and have no help but you,
for I am taking my life in my hand."
—ESTHER C:14–15

Queen Esther was a strong woman who risked her life to save her people from total annihilation. In reading her prayer, we look into the face of strength and resolve emerging from the pit of terror and despair. "Help me, who am alone and have no help but you." Keep this prayer handy when you wake up at three in the morning with fear gripping your heart and despair rattling your windowpane. Spoiler alert: Esther wins the day, and with God's help, so will you.

Esther C:12,14–16,23–25
Psalm 138:1–2ab,2cde–3,7c–8
Matthew 7:7–12

I trust in the LORD,
my soul trusts in his word.
My soul waits for the LORD.
—PSALM 130:5

Katharine Drexel was born into enormous wealth. Her parents insisted the money was on loan from God and meant to be shared with the poor. After Katharine cared for her parents until they died, she pondered what to do with her life. Her spiritual director advised, "Wait and pray." A trip out West inspired her to focus her energies and philanthropy on building schools for Native American and Black children.

Hoping to secure missionaries who would serve these populations, she visited Pope Leo XIII with her request. He suggested she become a missionary, so she founded the Sisters of the Blessed Sacrament, who continue her work to this day. We are all born with gifts and talents. Today, reflect on the gifts you will put to use for the good of others.

Ezekiel 18:21–28
Psalm 130:1–2,3–4,5–7a,7bc–8
Matthew 5:20–26

Saturday

MARCH 4

• ST. CASIMIR •

*Today you are making this agreement with the LORD
he is to be your God and you are to walk in his ways
and observe his statutes, commandments and decrees,
and to hearken to his voice.*
—DEUTERONOMY 26:17

The phrase "you will walk in his ways" sparks memories of
Luis Aparacio, aka "Little Louie." An amazing shortstop for
the Chicago White Sox, he was my boyhood hero. I studied
his every move. He would prowl the left half of the infield,
scooping up every ball that came his way. I spent hours in my
backyard throwing a rubber ball at our back wall to practice
my fielding so I could be just like Louie. I wanted to glide,
dart, dive, scoop, and throw "in his ways." It now seems to
me that observing God's commands is akin to my backyard
practice sessions—so that when it really matters, I will know
his voice and walk in his ways.

Deuteronomy 26:16–19
Psalm 119:1–2,4–5,7–8
Matthew 5:43–48

⇒ 98 ⇐

Sunday

MARCH 5

• SECOND SUNDAY OF LENT •

May your kindness, O LORD, be upon us
who have put our hope in you.
—PSALM 33:22

Too often people keep their lives on hold, waiting for
something new to happen. When I get the new job. . . .
When this big project is done. . . . Once we get the house
paid off . . . . When I lose ten pounds. . . . The point is to put
our hope in God—now! Today. In this minute and in the
situation I find myself in today. Now is the acceptable time.

Genesis 12:1–4a
Psalm 33:4–5,18–19,20,22
2 Timothy 1:8b–10
Matthew 17:1–9

"Stop judging and you will not be judged.
Stop condemning and you will not be condemned.
Forgive and you will be forgiven.
Give and gifts will be given to you."
—LUKE 6:37–38

What's your default position toward life? It may be hard to see it ourselves, but others around us could name our usual response to stress, threats, or the unfolding of life in general. A common response is judging. The problem with snap judgments is that we are often in no position to judge. We don't know all the facts and certainly can't know the content of another's heart. A healthier alternative is responding with compassionate curiosity. "I wonder why she said that?" Then I don't get locked into a malign view of life and others, and the circle of life can become a mutual offering of gifts such as respect, trust, even reverence for one another.

Daniel 9:4b–10
Psalm 79:8,9,11 and 13
Luke 6:36–38

MARCH 7

• ST. PERPETUA AND ST. FELICITY, MARTYRS •

Come now, let us set things right,
says the LORD:
Though your sins be like scarlet,
they may become white as snow.
—ISAIAH 1:18

I call them the "cringe inducers." These are the unfinished tasks, unmet promises, unfortunate words I blurted out in an awkward conversation and, of course, the actual harms I did to others that cause me to cringe when they pop into my mind, usually at three in the morning. They are the things I need to set right, and Lent is a great time to do just that. So, say a prayer, make a list, and set them right one at a time, starting today.

Isaiah 1:10,16–20
Psalm 50:8–9,16bc–17,21 and 23
Matthew 23:1–12

$\mathcal{W}ednesday$

MARCH 8

• ST. JOHN OF GOD •

Then the mother of the sons of Zebedee approached
Jesus with her sons
and did him homage, wishing to ask him
for something.
He said to her, "What do you wish?"
She answered him,
"Command that these two sons of mine sit,
one at your right and the other at your left,
in your kingdom."
—MATTHEW 20:17–19

It's like someone saying they have three months to live and a
coworker asks, "Do you think I could have your laptop?"
Jesus has just announced he will be mocked, scourged, and
condemned to death when the mother of James the Less and
John the Evangelist pressures him to see that her boys get
good jobs in this new kingdom he's been talking about.
Ouch! Reading today's Gospel has me reflecting on what I
ask of God and how I go about it.

Jeremiah 18:18–20
Psalm 31:5–6,14,15–16
Matthew 20:17–28

Thus says the LORD:
Cursed is the man who trusts in human beings,
who seeks his strength in flesh,
whose heart turns away from the LORD.
He is like a barren bush in the desert
that enjoys no change of season.
—JEREMIAH 17:5–6

What prophets do is hold a mirror before us to break through our blindness and help us see our lives clearly. Jeremiah uses the image of a barren bush stuck in a wasteland that bears no fruit to describe the person who turns away from God. He counters that with a description of those who trust in the Lord, comparing them to a tree planted beside a stream that withstands the drought and brings forth abundant fruit. Consider both images. Leafless bush in a wasteland or tree beside a running stream? Take your pick.

Jeremiah 17:5–10
Psalm 1:1–2, 3, 4, 6
Luke 16:19–31

Friday

MARCH 10

[Jesus said,] "Hear another parable.
There was a landowner who planted a vineyard,
put a hedge around it,
dug a wine press in it, and built a tower.
Then he leased it to tenants and went on a journey."
—MATTHEW 21:33

What parables do is entice us by story to stumble into
recognizing a personal blind spot. Today's parable involves
wily tenants who refused to give the landowner his due,
killed his servants, and planned to kill his son. Jesus' hearers
would surely have strong judgments about what happened to
that landowner, his servants, and his son. What they
stumbled into was that, in this story, *they* were the tenants. It
can take a lot to get us out of our set consciousness, which
we tend to think of as true reality. Ask God to help you
stumble into clarity about his will for you.

Genesis 37:3–4,12–13a,17b–28a
Psalm 105:16–17,18–19,20–21
Matthew 21:33–43,45–46

MARCH 11

So he got up and went back to his father.
While he was still a long way off,
his father caught sight of him, and was filled
with compassion.
He ran to his son, embraced him and kissed him.
His son said to him,
"Father, I have sinned against heaven and against you;
I no longer deserve to be called your son."
But his father ordered his servants,
"Quickly, bring the finest robe and put it on him;
put a ring on his finger and sandals on his feet."
—LUKE 15:20–23

If you struggle with perfectionism and the belief that you
have to earn your way to God's love, let this story seep into
your consciousness. Let that image of the father running
madly down the road because he spotted his wayward child
returning home sink into your soul. To me, this story is the
very heart of the Good News.

Micah 7:14–15,18–20
Psalm 103:1–2,3–4,9–10,11–12
Luke 15:1–3,11–32

Sunday

MARCH 12

• THIRD SUNDAY OF LENT •

Jesus answered and said to her,
"Everyone who drinks this water will be thirsty again;
but whoever drinks the water I shall give
will never thirst;
the water I shall give will become in him
a spring of water welling up to eternal life."
The woman said to him,
"Sir, give me this water, so that I may not be thirsty
or have to keep coming here to draw water."
—JOHN 4:13–15

A first step toward spiritual maturity is becoming comfortable with spiritual symbolism, and this reading from John is chock-full of it. In fact, Jesus and the Samaritan woman carry on an entire, intense conversation playing with the symbolism of water as God's own life poured out for us. The next time you take a drink of cool, clear water, think beyond the physical and imagine this is the "water welling up to eternal life" that Jesus promises. Cheers!

Exodus 17:3–7
Psalm 95:1–2,6–7,8–9
Romans 5:1–2,5–8
John 4:5–42 or 4:5–15,19b–26,39a,40–42

As the hind longs for running of water,
so my soul longs for you, O God.
—PSALM 42:2

Today we continue with the theme of yesterday's passage
about the Samaritan woman who came to the well seeking
living water. Today's passage is from one of the most
beautiful psalms describing human yearning for God. I am
grateful today for the people in my life who awakened and
nurtured my own longing for God, including my parents and
grandparents, as well as the priests, nuns, and lay teachers in
my parish who helped faith come alive. Who awakened
your faith?

2 Kings 5:1–15ab
Psalm 42:2,3; 43:3,4
Luke 4:24–30

Tuesday

MARCH 14

Then Peter approached Jesus and asked him,
"Lord, if my brother sins against me,
how often must I forgive him?
As many as seven times?"
Jesus answered, "I say to you, not seven times
but seventy-seven times."
—MATTHEW 18:21–22

Peter must have thought he was being quite magnanimous offering to forgive his brother seven times. In Jesus' eyes he was sure to win at being a good guy. But Jesus countered by saying you need to forgive seventy-seven times, which is to say, "infinity plus one." What Jesus was really saying is that forgiveness doesn't involve math. God, as Peter should have known from experience, puts no limits on his forgiveness, and neither should we. Sure, there are consequences of our sins, but that doesn't separate us from the love of God or the opportunity to repent, make amends, and return to God's good graces.

Daniel 3:25,34–43
Psalm 25:4–5ab,6 and 7bc,8–9
Matthew 18:21–35

MARCH 15

However, take care and be earnestly on your guard
not to forget the things your own eyes
have seen,
nor let them slip from your memory as long
as you live,
but teach them to your children and to your
children's children.
—DEUTERONOMY 4:9

A Scripture professor once told me the Bible is packed with people who were slow learners and fast forgetters. Think of Adam and Eve all the way through Peter and Paul. Today's message from Deuteronomy hits on a powerful remedy for us: don't forget the actions of God that your own eyes have seen, and make them known to the children in your care. Today, recall a time when you deeply felt the presence of God in your life and find a way (in person, via e-mail) to share that memory with a young person in your life.

Deuteronomy 4:1,5–9
Psalm 147:12–13,15–16,19–20
Matthew 5:17–19

This is what I commanded my people:
Listen to my voice;
then I will be your God and you shall be
my people.
Walk in all the ways that I command you,
so that you may prosper.
—JEREMIAH 7:23

How do we hear God's voice? The brilliant Sufi poet Rumi wrote, "Silence is the language of God, all else is poor translation." Modern culture does little to encourage silence in our lives. We have to work at finding a quiet place, and once we find it, we then have to quiet our mind and heart. It takes practice and persistence. Here's a tip: begin with a heartfelt prayer of praise. That will get your mind off your own concerns and open the door to the presence of God.

Jeremiah 7:23–28
Psalm 95:1–2,6–7,8–9
Luke 11:14–23

You shall love the Lord your God with all your heart,
with all your soul,
with all your mind,
and with all your strength.
—MARK 12:30

Sometimes at the end of a demanding day, my wife will ask how I'm feeling, and I'll say, "Scattered." At times like that I feel as though I left parts of me here and there all over the place throughout the day. My sense of integrity is shaken. That's when it helps to embrace a primary goal, in this case, to love the Lord my God with all my heart, soul, mind, and strength. It's like the Hokey-Pokey when you can finally "put your whole self in." And need I remind you, "That's what it's all about." Happy St. Paddy's Day!

Hosea 14:2–10
Psalm 81:6c–8a,8bc–9,10–11ab,14 and 17
Mark 12:28–34

What can I do with you, Ephraim?
What can I do with you, Judah?
Your piety is like a morning cloud,
like the dew that early passes away.
For this reason I smote them through the prophets,
I slew them by the words of my mouth;
For it is love that I desire, not sacrifice,
and knowledge of God rather than burnt offerings.
—HOSEA 6:4–6

There are times when we are uncertain of what God's will is in the moment. Don't let your uncertainty cause your faith to evaporate like the morning dew. You need not remain confused. "It is love that I desire," says the Lord. So stop, breathe, consider what you have come to know about God, and do what you judge to be the most loving thing.

Hosea 6:1–6
Psalm 51:3–4,18–19,20–21ab
Luke 18:9–14

*So a second time they called the man who
had been blind
and said to him, "Give God the praise!
We know that this man is a sinner."
He replied,
"If he is a sinner, I do not know.
One thing I do know is that I was blind and now I see."*
—JOHN 9:24–25

When I imagine myself in Gospel scenes, I sometimes cast myself as one of the Pharisees. Sure, it's tempting to stand with Jesus, cheering him on. But the lessons Jesus has for the Pharisees are ones that I need to learn as well. Today's lesson is all about seeing. The man born blind represents all of humanity. At some level we just don't see. And the sad part is how much energy we pharisees put into denying our blindness rather than letting ourselves see what Jesus so wants us to see.

1 Samuel 16:1b,6–7,10–13a
Psalm 23:1–3a,3b–4,5,6 (1)
Ephesians 5:8–14
John 9:1–41 or 9:1,6–9,13–17,34–38

Joseph her husband, since he was a righteous man,
yet unwilling to expose her to shame,
decided to divorce her quietly.
Such was his intention when, behold
the angel of the Lord appeared to him in a dream.
—MATTHEW 1:19–20

Well, one thing we know about Joseph is that he paid attention to his dreams. He was a man with a habit of expecting to hear from God. So, when an angel of the Lord appeared in a dream, Joseph knew to pay attention. His intention was to be a righteous man who would do God's will yet do no harm to Mary. His dream revealed that God's will in this situation was far different from what he supposed. In fact, he had a necessary role to play in bringing forth God's will by welcoming Mary, and Jesus, into his home.

2 Samuel 7:4–5a,12–14a,16
Psalm 89:2–3,4–5,27 and 29
Romans 4:13,16–18,22
Matthew 1:16,18–21,24a or Luke 2:41–51a

Jesus said to him, "Rise, take up your mat, and walk."
Immediately the man became well, took up his mat,
and walked.

Now that day was a sabbath.
So the Jews said to the man who was cured,
"It is the sabbath, and it is not lawful for you to
carry your mat."
—JOHN 5:8–10

Once again it comes down to what you see and what you look for. Jesus encountered the man who had been ill for thirty-eight years, asked him if he wanted to be well, and healed him on the spot. Self-appointed judgers were lurking about (aren't they always?), and did they see a man who had been ill and now was cured? No, all they could see was an infraction. Dear God, how often do I focus on the problem and miss the miracle?

Ezekiel 47:1–9,12
Psalm 46:2–3,5–6,8–9
John 5:1–16

MARCH 22

The LORD is near to all who call upon him,
to all who call upon him in truth.
—PSALM 145:18

What a comfort it is to know that when we cry out from the
depths of our hearts, God is near. Sometimes we don't let
ourselves recognize or feel what most deeply troubles us. We
cover it over with busyness, work, entertainment, worry
about trivial things, distractions of all sorts. It's when we call
upon him "in truth," that is, in the reality of our lives, that we
realize God is and always has been nearby.

Isaiah 49:8–15
Psalm 145:8–9,13cd–14,17–18
John 5:17–30

MARCH 23

• ST. TORIBIO DE MOGROVEJO, BISHOP •

They forgot the God who had saved them,
who had done great deeds in Egypt.
—PSALM 106:21

One of my early spiritual disappointments happened after I returned from an awe-inspiring retreat. I felt dismal that, after having had such a mountaintop experience of God's merciful love, I could so quickly return to feeling lost and alone. In time, I've come to see this as a pattern that many, if not most of us, experience. We have our moments of closeness to God followed by a return to our ordinary lives with our ordinary faults, foibles, and sins. What has helped is realizing that God is as much present in those valley times as he was on the mountaintop. God doesn't change, and that helps me stay the course even when the fog of forgetting starts to set in.

Exodus 32:7–14
Psalm 106:19–20,21–22,23
John 5:31–47

Friday

MARCH 24

Let us beset the just one, because he is obnoxious to us
he sets himself against our doings.
Reproaches us for transgressions of the law
and charges us with violations of our training.
He professes to have knowledge of God
and styles himself a child of the LORD.
—WISDOM 2:12–13

Is this why Jesus was put to death? Because he was annoying?
Had his inherent goodness become such a reproach that they
simply wanted him gone? The language in today's reading
sounds like something you'd hear on a middle-school
playground. "She thinks she's so good!" "He thinks he's so
much better than everyone else." "We've got to teach that
Goody-Two-shoes a lesson!" Bitterness and hate arise so
quickly when we feel threatened. Lord, teach us to hear your
word and witness your goodness anew, and harden not our
hearts.

Wisdom 2:1a,12–22
Psalm 34:17–18,19–20,21 and 23
John 7:1–2,10,25–30

MARCH 25

• THE ANNUNCIATION OF THE LORD •

Mary said, "Behold, I am the handmaid of the Lord.
May it be done to me according to your word."
Then the angel departed from her.
—LUKE 1:38

With her words "May it be done to me according to your word," Mary became the first disciple. Her yes to God was a wholehearted *yes*. It entailed a lifelong commitment in the face of uncertainty and fear. Many artistic renditions of the Annunciation depict Mary with the Scriptures open before her and a lily—symbol of a pure heart—nearby. This offers good advice for how to respond to difficult decisions in our own lives: open your mind to God's mind, and attune your heart to God's heart.

Isaiah 7:10–14; 8:10
Psalm 40:7–8a,8b–9,10,11
Hebrews 10:4–10
Luke 1:26–38

MARCH 26

• FIFTH SUNDAY OF LENT •

He cried out in a loud voice,
"Lazarus, come out!"
The dead man came out,
tied hand and foot with burial bands,
So Jesus said to them,
"Untie him and let him go."
—JOHN 11:43–44

Jesus' mission was to bring divine life into every corner of human life, including the arena of death itself. He begins by entering the world of grief, weeping openly at the tomb of his beloved friend Lazarus. He is moved to face down death itself, commanding, "Take the stone away." In a loud voice, which is a sign of God's presence, he calls Lazarus to come forth. Seeing his friend bound with burial cloths, Jesus speaks directly to death, echoing words Moses spoke to Pharoah, "Let him go!" Jesus does not merely join us in our human grief; he conquers death with God's own eternal life.

Ezekiel 37:12–14
Psalm 130:1–2,3–4,5–6,7–8
Romans 8:8–11
John 11:1–45 or 11:3–7, 17,20–27,33b–45

Even though I walk in the dark valley,
I fear no evil; for you are at my side. . . .
And I shall dwell in the house of the LORD
for years to come.
—PSALM 23:4, 6

Maybe you've seen a sign like this while driving along the highway: "If you lived in Happy Acres, you'd be home now!" The pitch is aimed at people eager to shorten their daily commute through horrible traffic. Psalm 23 offers a similar pitch: "If you dwelt in the house of the Lord (amid green pastures, conveniently located near right paths, long lease), you wouldn't have to travel all the way to the House of Fear (inconveniently located in the Valley of the Shadow of Death)." Psalm 23 seems to see only two options for where we can live: in fear, or in the Good Shepherd's house of goodness and mercy. Make yourself at home.

Daniel 13:1–9,15–17,19–30,33–62 or 13:41c–62
Psalm 23:1–3a,3b–4,5,6
John 8:1–11

With their patience worn out by the journey,
the people complained against God and Moses,
"Why have you brought us up from Egypt
to die in the desert?"
—NUMBERS 21:4–5

T. S. Eliot wrote that "April is the cruellest month," but for
those who live in northern regions, March is known as the
most dismal and tedious. Winter often lingers on, as
evidenced by dreary, sunless days and landscapes dotted with
stubborn, dirty snow mounds the consistency of iron. The
Hebrew people didn't have snow to contend with, but they
were worn out by their endless journey in trying conditions.
It's easy to lose heart and lose hope. Today, try taking the
longer view, not just of time—notice signs of spring peeking
out at the edges—but also purpose: we, too, are on a sacred
journey to a promised land, if only we keep the faith.

Numbers 21:4–9
Psalm 102:2–3,16–18,19–21
John 8:21–30

*Jesus said to those Jews who believed in him,
"If you remain in my word, you will truly
be my disciples,
and you will know the truth, and the truth
will set you free."*
—JOHN 8:31–32

You've probably heard the satiric version of Jesus' statement:
"The truth will set you free—but first it will make you
miserable." Facing the truth about ourselves wounds our ego,
highlights our weaknesses, and reveals that we're not as
purely wonderful as our inner PR agent claims we are.
Remaining in God's word requires that we accept reality as it
is, despite the discomfort it may bring. And as we grow in
wisdom and grace, we learn that the pain of facing hard
truths about ourselves is far preferable to the misery of living
the lie. Jesus sees who we are deep down and keeps calling us
forth to live in that truth.

Daniel 3:14–20,91–92,95
Daniel 3:52,53,54,55,56
John 8:31–42

Look to the LORD in his strength;
seek to serve him constantly.
Recall the wondrous deeds that he has wrought.
—PSALM 105:4–5

Sometimes we're so preoccupied with tomorrow's worries that we miss seeing the wondrous deeds God has wrought in our lives. Here's a way to help you seek his face sometime this Lent. Lay a piece of paper horizontally before you and draw a line from left to right. Choose a time frame of your life you want to review (a month, a year, the whole shebang) and write the start date on the left and the end date on the right. Ask the Holy Spirit to help as you focus your mind on significant events during that time. Put circles and squares where joys or challenges occurred. Then mark pluses where you felt the presence of God. Meditate on those events, recalling the wondrous deeds God has done.

Genesis 17:3–9
Psalm 105:4–5,6–7,8–9
John 8:51–59

The Jews picked up rocks to stone Jesus.
Jesus answered them, "I have shown you
many good works from my Father.
For which of these are you trying to stone me?"
—JOHN 10:31–32

All through this season of Lent, the Gospel readings grow
ominous with reports of the increasing threats against Jesus
from the religious leaders in Jerusalem. The burning question
that aggravates the leaders is, "Who does he think he is?"
Jesus points to the good works he has done as evidence that
who he is and what he is doing are of and from God. The
leaders only want to check his ID. Jesus' fate seems
inevitable. He travels back across the Jordan, to the place
where John first baptized. Where do you go to get grounded
when trouble looms?

Jeremiah 20:10–13
Psalm 18:2–3a,3bc–4,5–6,7
John 10:31–42

Saturday

APRIL 1

The chief priests and the Pharisees
convened the Sanhedrin and said,
"What are we going to do?
This man is performing many signs.
If we leave him alone, all will believe in him,
and the Romans will come
and take away both our land and our nation. . . ."
So from that day on they planned to kill him.
—JOHN 11:47–48, 53

Jesus has reached Jerusalem, and his words and popularity
alarm the members of the Sanhedrin. His growing popularity
has also come to the attention of Roman officials. Jesus'
believers wonder if he will risk entering Jerusalem. Like a
tragic opera, the stage is set. Jesus has grown more and more
aware that faithfulness to his mission could lead to his death.
Jesus retires to pray, then moves faithfully toward Jerusalem
and his destiny. Make time in the coming week to behold all
that is to transpire.

Ezekiel 37:21–28
Jeremiah 31:10,11–12abcd,13
John 11:45–56

Sunday

APRIL 2

"You who fear the Lord, praise him!
all you descendants of Jacob, give glory to him;
revere him, all you descendants of Israel!"
—PSALM 22:24

Show reverence. Holy Week begins, and the events that
signal our salvation are unfolding once again: the triumphant
entry into Jerusalem, the washing of the feet, the Last
Supper, the betrayals, the agony in the garden, Jesus'
surrender to his Father's will, the interrogations, the
scourging, the carrying of the cross, the weeping women at
the cross, the two thieves alongside him, the piercing, the
crying out, his death. Choose one of these events that speaks
to you and meditate on it today. With reverence.

PROCESSION:
Matthew 21:1–11

MASS:
Isaiah 50:4–7
Psalm 22:8–9,17–18,19–20,23–24
Philippians 2:6–11
Matthew 26:14—27:66 or 27:11–54

Monday

APRIL 3

I believe I shall see the bounty of the LORD
in the land of the living.
—PSALM 27:13

Years ago I saw a photo of a couple of elderly men sitting in
lawn chairs next to a sign saying, "This is *not* the Holy Hill."
Human beings are drawn to physical locations where we can
encounter God. We also then begin to regulate where God
can or cannot be found. Today's reading speaks of "the land
of the living," which refers to the temple in Jerusalem, where
the faithful had access to the life-giving presence of God.
Jesus is about to expand our notion of where God can be
found. His saving work renders every part of creation a place
to experience the presence of God—including the human
heart. Good news for the old guys in the lawn chairs—you're
already on the Holy Hill.

Isaiah 42:1–7
Psalm 27:1,2,3,13–14
John 12:1–11

APRIL 4

Peter said to him,
"Master, why can I not follow you now?
I will lay down my life for you."
Jesus answered, "Will you lay down your life for me?
Amen, amen, I say to you, the cock will not crow
before you deny me three times."
—JOHN 13:37–38

Peter always provides a mirror to my own struggles in following Jesus. He clearly loves Jesus and always longs to do the right thing. And, just as frequently, he stumbles badly. What Peter helps me with most is what to do after I stumble. Consider Judas versus Peter and how each man dealt with his betrayal of our Lord. Though Judas felt remorse, he despaired of God's mercy and took his life. Peter, for all his faults, kept coming back, always remorseful, clinging to hope, and willing to try one more time.

Isaiah 49:1–6
Psalm 71:1–2,3–4a,5ab–6ab,15 and 17
John 13:21–33,36–38

APRIL 5

• WEDNESDAY OF HOLY WEEK •

I gave my back to those who beat me,
my cheeks to those who plucked my beard.
—ISAIAH 50:6

Science is learning how trees communicate to help a
distressed tree through drought, disease, and other threats. If
one tree has been poisoned, the others collaborate to absorb
the toxins and release them.[2] Absorb and release. That is
what Jesus is about to do for us through his passion and
death. He will take on the sin of the world and relieve us of
sin's burden. He bears the outpouring of fear, hate, and utter
violence coming his way and releases us from bondage to
sin's ways. His dying and rising become the new pattern for
us, our new way.

Isaiah 50:4–9a
Psalm 69:8–10,21–22,31 and 33–34
Matthew 26:14–25

---

2.   https://www.smithsonianmag.com/science-nature/the-whispering-trees-180968084/.

So when he had washed their feet
and put his garments back on and reclined
at table again,
he said to them,
"Do you realize what I have done for you?"
—JOHN 13:12

Jesus' question to the disciples stands as the overriding question to us throughout the Triduum: "Do you realize what I have done for you?" Not just that you know it by rote, but to let the meaning of his actions become real, as real as washing feet. As we give ourselves over to these sacred rites from Holy Thursday through Easter Sunday, our task is to accompany Jesus at every step so that we may realize deep in our bones what he has done for us and continues to do for us. Let your guard down and walk beside him.

CHRISM MASS:
Isaiah 61:1–3a,6a,8b–9
Psalm 89:21–22,25 and 27
Revelation 1:5–8
Luke 4:16–21

EVENING MASS OF THE LORD'S SUPPER:
Exodus 12:1–8,11–14
Psalm 116:12–13,15–16bc,17–18
1 Corinthians 11:23–26
John 13:1–15

Yet it was our infirmities that he bore,
our sufferings that he endured.
—ISAIAH 53:4

In the course of his mortal life, Jesus went to every place that humans feel lost, forsaken, cut off from God, venturing even unto suffering and death. And to all those places and situations he brought God's love and compassion. He bore the pain of the human condition, seeking to reconcile all people, all places, all things with the Father, who created all and loves all. Today is the culmination of that part of the journey. "It is finished."

Isaiah 52:13—53:12
Psalm 31:2,6,12–13,15–16,17,25
Hebrews 4:14–16; 5:7–9
John 18:1—19:42

Saturday

APRIL 8

• HOLY SATURDAY •

*[The angel said,] "He is not here, for he has been raised just as he said.
Come and see the place where he lay."*
—MATTHEW 28:6

Tomorrow, families will gather, and some will be greeting a
newcomer or two—a niece's boyfriend, a cousin's fiancée, a
straggler who needed a place to land on Easter. And people
will rush to tell the family stories because—well, how could
this new person ever belong if he or she doesn't know the
stories that make us who we are? That's what tonight is all
about for Christians around the world. How can
newcomers—or any of us for that matter—know we belong
if we don't hear and tell the stories that make us who we are?
Listen closely. There's a lot to be shared.

VIGIL:
Genesis 1:1—2:2 or 1:1.26—31a
Psalm 104:1–2,5–6,10,12,13–14,24,35 or
33:4–5,6–7,12–13,20–22
Genesis 22:1–18 or 22:1–2,9a,10–13,15–18
Psalm 16:5,8,9–10,11
Exodus 14:15—15:1
Exodus 15:1–2,3–4,5–6,17–18
Isaiah 54:5–14
Psalm 30:2,4,5–6,11–12,13
Isaiah 55:1–11

Isaiah 12:2–3,4,5–6
Baruch 3:9–15,32—4:4
Psalm 19:8,9,10,11
Ezekiel 36:16–17a,18–28
Psalm 42:3,5; 43:3,4 or Isaiah
12:2–3,4bcd,5–6 or Psalm
51:12–13,14–15,18–19
Romans 6:3–11
Psalm 118:1–2,16–17,22–23
Matthew 28:1–10

Sunday

APRIL 9

• EASTER SUNDAY OF THE RESURRECTION OF THE LORD •

To him all the prophets bear witness,
that everyone who believes in him
will receive forgiveness of sins through his name.
—ACTS 10:43

Here we are on Easter Sunday. After the intensity of the past
week, especially the past three days, it can seem like a
letdown. So much happened! What does it all mean? I find
this quote from the wise Fr. Ronald Rolheiser, OMI, a
perceptive assessment of what we've witnessed during Holy
Week: "Jesus' death washes everything clean, each of us and
the whole world. It heals everything, understands everything,
and forgives everything—despite every ignorance, weakness,
infidelity, and betrayal on our part."[3] Praise to you, Lord Jesus
Christ!

Acts 10:34a,37–43
Psalm 118:1–2,16–17,22–23
Colossians 3:1–4 or 1 Corinthians 5:6b–8
John 20:1–9 or Matthew 28:1–10 or, at an afternoon or evening Mass, Luke 24:13–35

3.   https://ronrolheiser.com/the-meaning-of-jesus-death/#.YF33Xi2cZTY.

⇉ 134 ⇇

Keep me safe, O God, for in you I take refuge.

> *You will show me the path to life,*
> *fullness of joys in your presence,*
> *the delights at your right hand forever.*
> —PSALM 16:1,11

How do we know Jesus is risen? We experience him in prayer, in the gathering at the table, in the word of God proclaimed, in the breaking of the bread. We feel his presence when we experience awe or unexpected grace. When we forgive or are forgiven. If we have the eyes to see, we recognize him in the people we encounter in the course of our day. We feel his real presence and know that he is with us, keeping us safe, showing us the path to eternal life.

Acts 2:14,22–33
Psalm 16:1–2a and 5,7–8,9–10,11
Matthew 28:8–15

Tuesday

APRIL 11

• TUESDAY WITHIN THE OCTAVE OF EASTER •

He loves justice and right;
of the kindness of the LORD the earth is full.
—PSALM 33:5

When you hear the word *God*, does the word *kindness* leap to
mind? Sadly, for many people the answer would be no. But
the psalmist assures us that the earth is full of the Lord's
kindness. If you take the time to think about it, you're likely
to recall numerous times when you've been touched by God's
tender care. So take time today to make a gratitude list,
acknowledging the many ways God's kindness fills
your world.

Acts 2:36–41
Psalm 33:4–5,18–19,20 and 22
John 20:11–18

So they set out at once and returned to Jerusalem
where they found gathered together
the Eleven.
—LUKE 24:33

The two discouraged disciples were walking away from
Jerusalem. In deep desolation they were fleeing the scene of
Jesus' scandalous imprisonment, suffering, and crucifixion.
But the risen Jesus didn't leave them. He joined them on the
road and, through word, presence, and gesture, responded so
effectively to their confusion that "their hearts were burning
within them." It was in the breaking of the bread that they
recognized him. And so they turned around. They set out at
once and rejoined the disciples in Jerusalem, ready for
whatever would come next. Recall a time when your heart
burned within you.

Acts 3:1–10
Psalm 105:1–2,3–4,6–7,8–9
Luke 24:13–35

APRIL 13

[Jesus] said to them,
"Thus it is written that the Christ would suffer
and rise from the dead on the third day
and that repentance, for the forgiveness of sins,
would be preached in his name
to all the nations, beginning from Jerusalem.
You are witnesses of these things."
—LUKE 24:46–48

We, too, are witnesses of these things. We have witnessed their unfolding, perhaps many times, in the sacred rites of Holy Week. And we have tasted the truth of Jesus' dying and rising whenever we chose to die to ourselves—our selfishness, our pride, our fear, our errant wants. And when we forgive or are forgiven, we proclaim his name in our words and deeds. Amen, alleluia.

Acts 3:11–26
Psalm 8:2ab and 5,6–7,8–9
Luke 24:35–48

Friday

APRIL 14

• FRIDAY WITHIN THE OCTAVE OF EASTER •

They laid hands on Peter and John
and put them in custody.
—ACTS 4:3

Imagine being a follower of Jesus when it was dangerous to do so. After Peter cured a man who was crippled, he and John were preaching to the crowds gathered in the temple courtyard. The priests, temple guard, and Sadducees laid hands on them and arrested them. Knowing what had recently happened to Jesus, they knew the same fate could easily befall them. But instead of shying away from danger, Peter stood up and boldly proclaimed the resurrection of Jesus. There are Christians today around the globe who are persecuted for their faith. They deserve our awareness, prayers, solidarity, and support.

Acts 4:1–12
Psalm 118:1–2 and 4,22–24,25–27a
John 21:1–14

———————————

But later, as the Eleven were at table,
he appeared to them
and rebuked them for their unbelief
and hardness of heart.
—MARK 16:14

I really feel for the apostles. Imagine yourself in that
nebulous time between Easter and Pentecost—stunned, still
trying to comprehend what happened after Jesus died. And
then Jesus appears and rebukes them for their hardness of
heart. My heart, too, becomes hardened when I feel
threatened and unsure. Jesus' recommended cure is to "go
into the whole world and proclaim the gospel." In other
words, get up and get busy living the life you are called to.
Sometimes we need to hunker down. But that's not where
we're meant to stay. Our mission is to actively engage the
world, using our gifts to make the Good News evident to
those we encounter. Maybe we first need our own Pentecost.

Acts 4:13–21
Psalm 118:1 and 14–15ab,16–18,19–21
Mark 16:9–15

APRIL 16

• SECOND SUNDAY OF EASTER (OR SUNDAY OF DIVINE MERCY) •

*They devoted themselves
to the teaching of the apostles
and to the communal life,
to the breaking of bread and to the prayers.
Awe came upon everyone,
and many wonders and signs were done
through the apostles.*
—ACTS 2:42–43

"Awe came upon everyone." This passage about life in the early days of the church can leave me envious. I recall the days when our parish went all in for a renewal program and was full of life and purpose. I get envious because that level of awe and hope is hard to sustain. But the other day I dropped into daily Mass and saw the school kids gathered and singing the entrance hymn with gusto. And awe is once again in the air.

Acts 2:42–47
Psalm 118:2–4,13–15,22–24
1 Peter 1:3–9
John 20:19–31

Nicodemus said to him,
"How can a man once grown old be born again?"
—JOHN 3:4

Today's Gospel says Nicodemus came to see Jesus at night,
which is appropriate because he sure was in the dark about
what Jesus was trying to tell him. Nicodemus provides an
example of why the Scriptures should be taken seriously but
not always literally. He resolutely refused to see that Jesus was
talking about a spiritual reality when he said we must be born
from above. We all have our blind spots, so it's important to
come at Scripture—especially the words of Jesus—with a
certain amount of humility, asking the Holy Spirit to help us
see what our physical eyes alone cannot see. Keeping a good
Bible commentary handy couldn't hurt, either.

Acts 4:23–31
Psalm 2:1–3,4–7a,7b–9
John 3:1–8

Tuesday

APRIL 18

And he has made the world firm,
not to be moved.
Your throne stands firm from of old;
from everlasting you are, O LORD.
—PSALM 93:1B–2A

A friend told me about the day he lived through the 1989 San Francisco earthquake. He was a sportswriter covering the World Series game when Candlestick Park "began shaking like a bowl of Jell-O." Days later he was still feeling the emotional aftershock. We are all looking for solid ground in our lives physically, emotionally, and spiritually. God created a world and made it firm. God also gives us a life of purpose and meaning, which can keep us stable and grounded, despite life's unpredictability. Spending time in prayer daily helps us get in touch with that solid place on which to build a worthy life.

Acts 4:32–37
Psalm 93:1ab,1cd–2,5
John 3:7b–15

Wednesday

APRIL 19

God so loved the world that he gave his
only-begotten Son,
so that everyone who believes in him
might not perish
but might have eternal life.
—JOHN 3:16

This is the core message, the gospel in miniature. It's a story that begins and ends in compassion, generosity, and love. We have the author of the Gospel of John to thank for putting this all so concisely, a statement of God's intention and Jesus' mission. Whenever you feel confused as to what we believe, read this verse and repeat as necessary. It's a faith compass you can rely on.

Acts 5:17–26
Psalm 34:2–3,4–5,6–7,8–9
John 3:16–21

Taste and see how good the LORD is;
blessed the man who takes refuge in him.
—PSALM 34:9

Our faith in Jesus is incarnational. That means we receive it and experience it in our bodies, right here and right now. In fact, when we gather to worship, we become the body of Christ. As spring unfolds, try this spiritual practice: use all your senses to become aware of the goodness of the Lord. You might see the trees starting to put forth leaves, feel the touch of a breeze, smell the blossoms bursting forth, listen to the birds chattering, take time to really taste your food at your next meal. After each experience, say, "Thank you, God, for the gift of sight, smell, sound, touch, taste."

Acts 5:27–33
Psalm 34:2 and 9,17–18,19–20
John 3:31–36

Friday

APRIL 21

• ST. ANSELM, BISHOP AND DOCTOR OF THE CHURCH •

"Have nothing to do with these men, and let them go.
For if this endeavor or this activity is of human origin,
it will destroy itself.
But if it comes from God, you will not be able
to destroy them;
you may even find yourself fighting against God."
—ACTS 5:38–39

St. Anselm, a Benedictine monk of the eleventh and twelfth centuries, is admired for his theological scholarship as well as his patience, gentleness, and teaching skill. A natural leader, he was elected prior and eventually abbot of the monastery at Bec in Normandy. Like the apostles referred to in today's reading, as Archbishop of Canterbury he faced conflict from political leaders. Reading the lives of the saints shows us that every life has challenges and that each of us can receive the graces we need, as we need them.

Acts 5:34–42
Psalm 27:1,4,13–14
John 6:1–15

APRIL 22

"Brothers, select from among you seven reputable men,
filled with the Spirit and wisdom,
whom we shall appoint to this task."
—ACTS 6:3

The apostles faced growing pains. The community of believers was growing rapidly, but there were discrepancies in the daily distribution of food, and the widows of the Hellenists were being neglected. Organizations will always need to respond to change, and today's reading describes the essential qualities needed in anyone practicing ministry: attunement to the Holy Spirit and wisdom, which is seeing with the eyes of Christ. We may not face the same challenges today, but the qualities that were necessary for those serving in the early church remain constant.

Acts 6:1–7
Psalm 33:1–2,4–5,18–19
John 6:16–21

APRIL 23

• THIRD SUNDAY OF EASTER •

You will show me the path to life,
abounding joy in your presence,
the delights at your right hand forever.
—PSALM 16:11A

Many young people I meet feel great urgency about finding their path in life. They want meaning and connection and purpose, and they wonder how they'll find a life that satisfies their deepest needs. Today's Gospel reading recalls the disciples on the road to Emmaus. They had chosen that path as an escape from the danger and disappointment they experienced in Jerusalem. Jesus came, walked with them, and pointed them back to where their true happiness would be found—in fellowship with the disciples. It's inevitable that we'll all be confused at times, but we can have confidence that if we are lost, Jesus will find us and show us the path we're actually looking for.

Acts 2:14,22–33
Psalm 16:1–2,5,7–8,9–10,11 (11a)
1 Peter 1:17–21
Luke 24:13–35

Monday

APRIL 24

• ST. FIDELIS OF SIGMARINGEN, PRIEST AND MARTYR •

"What can we do to accomplish the works of God?"
Jesus answered and said to them,
"This is the work of God, that you believe in
the one he sent."
—JOHN 6:28–29

What does it mean to "believe in the one he sent"? Believing
is a process, not a once-for-all outcome. It is an ongoing
activity that God initiates by offering the gift of faith, and we
must open up to it daily. Here's one suggestion for a daily
practice: Begin with praise. Immerse yourself in gratitude.
Read the holy word. Imagine yourself alongside Jesus as he
preaches, teaches, heals, and reveals. Pray for the graces you
need this day. Thank him when the day is done.

Acts 6:8–15
Psalm 119:23–24,26–27,29–30
John 6:22–29

≥ 149 ≤

APRIL 25

• ST. MARK, EVANGELIST •

Jesus appeared to the Eleven and said to them:
"Go into the whole world
and proclaim the Gospel to every creature.
Whoever believes and is baptized will be saved."
—MARK 16:15–16

There are people we encounter who are quiet proclaimers of the Gospel. They proclaim by their example and their actions. They proclaim by their kindness and their care. They proclaim by their confident trust that "all will be well." And they proclaim best by their trust in the intervention of the Holy Spirit at every turn. Pay attention today to the quiet proclaimers you meet.

1 Peter 5:5b–14
Psalm 89:2–3,6–7,16–17
Mark 16:15–20

*"But I told you that although you have seen me,
you do not believe."*
—JOHN 6:36

For Jesus, belief means more than giving intellectual assent. It involves a wholehearted, full-bodied yes that reorients one's entire life. So why is it so hard to accept the invitation to live as God calls us to live? Maybe it's because we unconsciously cling to old ideas: I'm the only one who can really take care of me; the only thing that will fill the emptiness inside me is shopping, alcohol, work, worry, etc. These kinds of ideas have been subconsciously directing our lives for years. Later in this reading from John, Jesus says, "I will not reject anyone who comes to me." Take his offer seriously. Pray daily for the willingness to let go of anything that keeps you from him, and God will not reject you.

Acts 8:1b–8
Psalm 66:1–3a,4–5,6–7a
John 6:35–40

Thursday

APRIL 27

*"No one can come to me unless the Father who
sent me draw him."*
—JOHN 6:44

We learn something significant about the nature of God the
Father in today's Gospel. The Father will draw us to Jesus. He
won't command. He won't coerce. He won't use scare tactics.

An excellent professor I had on my way to becoming a
spiritual director, Bill Creed, SJ, offered a helpful distinction
to make when discerning if something is God's will or
otherwise. He said, "Think of when you feel driven toward a
decision, or when you feel drawn toward it. If it's driven, it's
likely not of God. If you feel drawn, it is more likely to be of
God." I have used that test often, and it has never failed me.

Acts 8:26–40
Psalm 66:8–9,16–17,20
John 6:44–51

• ST. PETER CHANEL, PRIEST AND MARTYR • ST. LOUIS GRIGNION DE
MONTFORT, PRIEST •

On his journey, as he was nearing Damascus,
a light from the sky suddenly flashed around him.
He fell to the ground and heard a voice saying to him,
"Saul, Saul, why are you persecuting me?"
He said, "Who are you, sir?"
The reply came, "I am Jesus, whom you are persecuting.
Now get up and go into the city and you will be
told what you must do."
—ACTS 9:3–6

What a turnaround! Today's reading begins, "Saul, still
breathing murderous threats against the disciples of the Lord"
and ends with Paul, days later, "proclaiming Jesus in the
synagogues." How does a life turn around so completely?
Jesus always had the knack of asking just the right question at
the right time. What is he asking you today?

Acts 9:1–20
Psalm 117:1bc,2
John 6:52–59

APRIL 29

• ST. CATHERINE OF SIENA, VIRGIN AND DOCTOR OF THE CHURCH •

How shall I make a return to the LORD
for all the good he has done for me?
—PSALM 116:12

One of the Spiritual Exercises of St. Ignatius of Loyola has the retreatant answer these three questions: What have I done for the Lord? What am I doing for the Lord? What ought I do for the Lord? These questions help put my response to God's goodness in context over time. Recalling times when I've served the Lord well can bring fresh inspiration. Assessing my current level of service can provide a wake-up call if I have slacked off. Looking to the future helps me make the adjustments needed. Conducting such a review under the loving gaze of Christ reminds me I do none of this unaided.

Acts 9:31–42
Psalm 116:12–13,14–15,16–17
John 6:60–69

Sunday

APRIL 30

• FOURTH SUNDAY OF EASTER •

"A thief comes only to steal and slaughter and destroy;
I came so that they might have life
and have it more abundantly."
—JOHN 10:10

Years ago, I saw a bumper sticker that said: "Jesus is coming;
everybody look busy!" At first, I laughed. Then I began to
question what made me so uncomfortable to think of Jesus
returning. I realized that a part of me fears that Jesus is
coming only to condemn. Yet we have Jesus' own words
telling why he came—so that we may have abundant life.
The joy inherent in that new life is what I've always desired.
Ironically, what often keeps me from enjoying life more
abundantly is the false belief that I need to constantly
keep busy.

Acts 2:14a,36–41
Psalm 23:1–3a,3b–4,5,6 (1)
1 Peter 2:20b–25
John 10:1–10

Monday

MAY 1

• ST. JOSEPH THE WORKER •

"If then God gave them the same gift he gave to us
when we came to believe in the Lord Jesus Christ,
who was I to be able to hinder God?"
—ACTS 11:17

Peter finally learned a lesson. Earlier, he and other disciples were sometimes quick to discriminate as to who was worthy of God's blessing. In today's reading, speaking of the gentiles seeking to follow Jesus, Peter says, "The Spirit told me to accompany them without discriminating." A foundational lesson of our faith that goes all the way back to Abraham (and even earlier!) is this: "Let God be God." Who are we to hinder what God is doing in the world by being closed-minded?

Acts 11:1–18
Psalm 42:2–3; 43:3–4
John 10:11–18 or, for Memorial, Genesis 1:26—2:3 or Colossians 3:14–15,17,23–24 /
Matthew 13:54–58

Tuesday

MAY 2

• ST. ATHANASIUS, BISHOP AND DOCTOR OF THE CHURCH •

"The Father and I are one."
—JOHN 10:30

Who do we include when we say the word "us"? More important, who do we automatically exclude? That was the dilemma for the mostly Jewish early followers of Jesus when non-Jewish people were drawn to follow Jesus. It was a problem for Peter and other leaders of the early church, as it has been a problem for humans long before and ever since. We seem to be hardwired to choose sides and look askance at those who, through birth or custom, appear different from us. Jesus says, "The Father and I are one." Jesus frequently preached that we are all meant to be one. Not the same, but one in unity. That's what we practice when we participate in the Eucharist—Holy Communion. Who do you include when say "us"? Who do you leave out?

Acts 11:19–26
Psalm 87:1b–3,4–5,6–7
John 10:22–30

Wednesday

MAY 3

• ST. PHILIP AND ST. JAMES, APOSTLES •

The heavens declare the glory of God;
and the firmament proclaims his handiwork.
Day pours out the word to day,
and night to night imparts knowledge.
—PSALM 19:2–3

Being a city kid, I was literally stunned the first time I walked
out into the sea of stars in Northern Michigan. The heavens
weren't the only ones declaring the glory of God. My whole
family was wrapped up in amazement as we raised our heads
in awe and praise for the God who created this splendor. We
felt at once small and inconsequential in the grand story of
life, and also singularly blessed to stand in this place at this
time on such a still, clear night when all that we could do was
lift our hearts in praise. The heavens declared God's glory;
we swam in the evidence.

1 Corinthians 15:1–8
Psalm 19:2–3,4–5
John 14:6–14

MAY 4

So Paul got up, motioned with his hand, and said,
"Fellow children of Israel and you others
who are God-fearing, listen."
—ACTS 13:16

St. Paul was invited by the synagogue officials in Antioch to offer a word of exhortation for the people. And, wow, did he deliver. Paul began with a sweeping account of how God chose the people of Israel, led them out of bondage to the Promised Land, gave them kings and prophets to guide them, and promised them a savior. Paul continued, linking that familiar prelude to the arrival of John the Baptist, who prepared the way for Jesus. Paul was making the case that Jesus is not a detour away from God's plan but the fulfillment of God's plan. What's more, his message is meant for all.

Acts 13:13–25
Psalm 89:2–3,21–22,25 and 27
John 13:16–20

MAY 5

"Do not let your hearts be troubled.
You have faith in God; have faith also in me."
—JOHN 14:1

I don't know about you, but the times I goof up the most are when I let my heart be troubled and I fail to exercise my faith. Worry gets the better of me. I begin to see enemies everywhere. Fear abounds. Self-pity follows. My vision of life narrows and hope fades. What I can do instead is stop, breathe, put my trouble in God's hands, talk to a positive friend, help someone who needs it, and recall how often my previous worries vanished when I invited God in and simply did the next right thing in front of me.

Acts 13:26–33
Psalm 2:6–7,8–9,10–11ab
John 14:1–6

Saturday

MAY 6

Philip said to Jesus,
"Master, show us the Father, and that will be
enough for us."
—JOHN 14:8

Philip suffered what many of us suffer: wrongheaded ideas
about God. Think about it: how many people talk about God
as if he's a traffic cop, lying in wait to catch us doing
something wrong? Or God as fairy godmother, granting
wishes on demand. Or, a popular one these days, God as
absentee landlord, never there when you need him. Philip
wanted Jesus to reduce God to human size. But wasn't that
what God was doing through the Incarnation? "Here I am,"
replies Jesus, who not only reveals the Father but also models
how to approach him through prayer and service to others.

Acts 13:44–52
Psalm 98:1,2–3ab,3cd–4
John 14:7–14

Sunday

MAY 7

• FIFTH SUNDAY OF EASTER •

Lord, let your mercy be on us, as we place our trust in you.
—PSALM 33:22

Have you ever considered the difference between faith and trust? A fellow parishioner taught us a lesson about that at a faith-sharing group one evening. "I was praying with closed fists," he said. "I always believed God could help me, but even though I kept praying for his help, nothing changed. Then I looked down at my hands and realized that all the while I was telling God, 'I turn this problem over to you,' I was tightly clenching my fists. Outwardly, I was expressing my inner lack of trust. I'd always believed in God, but that day I learned to trust him. I opened my hands and prayed, and I knew I was finally turning the problem over to God."

Acts 6:1–7
Psalm 33:1–2,4–5,18–19 (22)
1 Peter 2:4–9
John 14:1–12

*"The Advocate, the Holy Spirit
whom the Father will send in my name—
he will teach you everything
and remind you of all that I told you."*
—JOHN 14:26

Three things to keep in mind about the Holy Spirit: (1) The
Holy Spirit is at work in the world and at work in you. (2)
The Holy Spirit is our Advocate, the one who is always
looking out for our best interests. (3) The Holy Spirit will
reawaken you to the wisdom that has already been placed in
your heart. The summation of these truths is, "Turn to the
Holy Spirit daily, in good times and bad, and you will be led
to a life of joy, hope, and deep satisfaction."

Acts 14:5–18
Psalm 115:1–2,3–4,15–16
John 14:21–26

Tuesday

MAY 9

*They stoned Paul and dragged him out of the city
supposing that he was dead.
But when the disciples gathered around him,
he got up and entered the city.*

—ACTS 14:19–20

The early days of the church were both invigorating and
challenging. Many were drawn to the preaching of Paul and
the apostles. Many others (both Jews and gentiles) were
irate, finding the message of Jesus disruptive and threatening.
This put the apostles in a dangerous situation as they tried to
follow Jesus' command to "preach the Good News to the
whole world." We have our own challenges today, not only
bringing Christ's message out to the world but also
effectively communicating that message closer to home,
including within our own homes and parishes. May we have
the strength and resilience of St. Paul.

Acts 14:19–28
Psalm 145:10–11,12–13ab,21
John 14:27–31a

MAY 10

• ST. DAMIEN DE VEUSTER, PRIEST •

"I am the vine, you are the branches.
Whoever remains in me and I in him will bear
much fruit."
—JOHN 15:5

Jesus leaned heavily on parables, allegory, and analogy to convey the spiritual truths he came to proclaim. Today's Gospel highlights the parable of the vine and the branches, one of the most effective figures of speech he used to describe our relationship to him and to the Father. The Father is the ground from which the vine emerges. The vine draws life from the ground, and that very life flows into the branches (us!). When we remain attached and open to the vine (through prayer, sacraments, and willingness), our life flourishes. Spend time today meditating on this parable in your heart.

Acts 15:1–6
Psalm 122:1–2, 3–4ab, 4cd–5
John 15:1–8

MAY 11

*"I have told you this so that
my joy might be in you and
your joy might be complete."*
—JOHN 15:11

Complete joy. Do I even know what that would feel like? So
often when I feel joy—especially since I've reached
adulthood—there is always a niggling, worrisome voice of
fear within that robs me of the completeness Jesus would
have me relish. The extent of my joy depends on the quality
of my spiritual condition. If I'm surrendering all to God early
and often, my capacity for joy grows. When I'm holding
back out of fear, self-centeredness, or grandiosity, my joy
response wanes. It's my choice each day. Lord, today I ask
you to help me choose you, thereby choosing joy.

Acts 15:7–21
Psalm 96:1–2a,2b–3,10
John 15:9–11

• ST. NEREUS AND ST. ACHILLEUS, MARTYRS * ST. PANCRAS, MARTYR •

"This is my commandment: love one another
as I love you."
—JOHN 15:12

When I was twenty, I had a crisis of faith. I had been on one life path and realized it was not for me. I felt lost and without purpose. My prayer life was a desert. I clung to one remnant of my faith, Jesus' words: "Love one another." I signed up to work as a camp counselor for young boys who were wards of the state. I was responsible for the sixteen boys ages five through nine of B Cabin. As duty turned to care, and care turned to affection, my gratitude for the youngsters in B Cabin became, to my surprise, selfless love. Over the summer, my faith returned slowly, nourished by the daily actions of love required to ensure the well-being and happiness of the little lads in my care.

Acts 15:22–31
Psalm 57:8–9,10 and 12
John 15:12–17

Saturday

MAY 13

• OUR LADY OF FATIMA •

When they came to Mysia, they tried to go on
into Bithynia,
but the Spirit of Jesus did not allow them,
so they crossed through Mysia and came down
to Troas.
—ACTS 16:7–8

At every step, the followers of Jesus practiced discernment—that is, listening deeply to the Spirit to guide them on their mission. Sometimes that discernment caused them to say no to what seemed like a good plan. Tomorrow is Mother's Day. For those who are mothers or serve in that role, take time to discern what you should say no to today and tomorrow. Sure, there's always more that can be done, but maybe the Spirit of Jesus is calling you to rest, prayer, and relaxed enjoyment of your role.

Acts 16:1–10
Psalm 100:1b–2,3,5
John 15:18–21

Always be ready to give an explanation
to anyone who asks you for a reason for your hope,
but do it with gentleness and reverence.
—1 PETER 3:15–16

Sometimes the person most in need of a reason for our hope is ourselves. "Why even bother?" we might sigh after a rough day when all our efforts seem to have come to naught. Peter recommends we offer our explanation with gentleness and reverence, which is ironic because pre-betrayal Peter was long on exuberance but short on gentleness. In fear, we might try to shore up our hope with a scolding pep talk that won't help in the least. Instead, in reverence, imagine the gaze of Christ—gentle, kind, full of compassion—landing on you. You will not only know about hope, you will experience a transfusion of it from its source.

Acts 8:5–8,14–17
Psalm 66:1–3,4–5,6–7,16,20
1 Peter 3:15–18
John 14:15–21

*"If you consider me a believer in the Lord,
come and stay at my home," and she prevailed upon us.*
—ACTS 16:15

Lydia, a dealer in purple (aka royal) cloth, heard Paul and his
companions preaching in Philippi and "opened her heart."
She also opened her home, inviting Paul and company to
stay at her presumably fine estate. Today is the feast of St.
Isidore, the farmer, a poor man who, with his wife, had a
seemingly miraculous stew pot that never ran out, no matter
how many hungry travelers found their way to the couple's
home. True faith leads to hospitality, whether we're opening
our homes, our wallets, or our hearts. Pray today to freely
receive grace so you may freely share it with those you'll
encounter.

Acts 16:11–15
Psalm 149:1b–2,3–4,5–6a and 9b
John 15:26—16:4a

MAY 16

"Now I am going to the one who sent me,
and not one of you asks me, 'Where are you going?'
But because I told you this, grief has filled your hearts.
But I tell you the truth, it is better for you that I go.
For if I do not go, the Advocate will not come to you."
—JOHN 16:5–7

Grief can be the prelude to the coming of the Holy Spirit in our lives. In our loss—of certainty, comfort, the way things were—we have room for the new. New ideas, new understanding, fresh hope emanating from a greater depth. Grief must be given its due in terms of time, attention, and willingness to have its way with us. Grief carves out the space within us in which the Holy Spirit can "fill our hearts and enkindle in us the fire of God's love."

Acts 16:22–34
Psalm 138:1–2ab,2cde–3,7c–8
John 16:5–11

Then Paul stood up at the Areopagus and said:
"You Athenians, I see that in every respect
you are very religious.
For as I walked around looking carefully at your shrines,
I even discovered an altar inscribed,
'To an Unknown God.'
What therefore you unknowingly worship,
I proclaim to you."
—ACTS 17:22–23

Imagine St. Paul arriving in a new country, preaching about the one true God to people who had dozens of gods. Where do you begin? Paul found his opening at the shrine To an Unknown God, for he proclaimed the God the people had longed for but did not yet know. Today, we stand with Paul, trying in our own ways to proclaim the living God to others who have yet to be effectively introduced.

Acts 17:15,22—18:1
Psalm 148:1–2,11–12,13,14
John 16:12–15

MAY 18

• THE ASCENSION OF THE LORD * •

Amen, amen, I say to you,
you will weep and mourn while the world rejoices;
you will grieve, but your grief will become joy.
—JOHN 16:20

Years back I heard a homily about how people handle both good and "seemingly bad" news. That phrase, "seemingly bad," caught my attention. The homilist told about times he was disappointed with a situation, only to realize later that it all turned out for the best. Not every difficult situation turns out wonderfully. But often, a situation one may consider "the end of the world" turns out far better than could ever be imagined. That's how it was for the Apostles after Jesus died. So stay "trust-ready," always open to the reality that God is at work in the world, including your world.

Acts 18:1–8
Psalm 98:1,2–3ab,3cd–4
John 16:16–20

FOR PROVINCES CELEBRATING THE
ASCENSION OF THE LORD
Acts 1:1–11
Psalm 47:2–3,6–7,8–9
Ephesians 1:17–23
Matthew 28:16–20

Jesus said to his disciples:
"Amen, amen, I say to you, you will weep and mourn,
while the world rejoices;
you will grieve, but your grief will become joy."
—JOHN 16:20

Liturgically, we are in an in-between time, between Jesus' Ascension and Pentecost, when the Holy Spirit will descend, bringing courage and joy to the apostles. But for now, the apostles are locked away in the upper room, fearful and confused. There are days, even stretches of days, when we can feel that way. We have our own versions of the upper room—maybe just pulling the covers over our head and hitting the snooze alarm one more time. Thankfully, we have also experienced Pentecost over the years. We know that the apparent disappearance of Jesus is temporary and that the Spirit will soon usher us back to courage and joy.

Acts 18:9–18
Psalm 47:2–3,4–5,6–7
John 16:20–23

All you peoples, clap your hands;
shout to God with cries of gladness.
For the LORD, the Most High, the awesome,
is the great king over all the earth.
—PSALM 47:2–3

On some days life feels wonderful, God is in his heaven, and all is right with the world—at least our little corner of it. If you're feeling that way today, great! Relish the feeling for it is from God. If not, recall a time when you felt especially alive, that the day was one big gift from God, and your heart was filled with gratitude. Savor that memory and make that your prayer today. Life is a gift. Receive it, embrace it, live it with gratitude.

Acts 18:23–28
Psalm 47:2–3,8–9,10
John 16:23b–28

Sunday

MAY 21

*[Jesus said,] "It is not for you to know the times or seasons
that the Father has established by his own authority.
But you will receive power when the Holy Spirit
comes upon you."*
—ACTS 1:7–8

Imagine hearing those parting words of Jesus: "You will
receive power when the Holy Spirit comes upon you." What
power would you want to receive? The power to make your
kids behave? Get your boss transferred, preferably to a
remote location? The power to get a raise, improve your
memory, lose thirty pounds in three weeks? Or how about
the power to know and do God's will? The power to forgive
those who do you wrong? The power to stand up for just
treatment of others? The Holy Spirit is coming bearing gifts.
What's on your wish list?

FOR PROVINCES CELEBRATING THE
ASCENSION OF THE LORD
Acts 1:1–11
Psalm 47:2–3,6–7,8–9
Ephesians 1:17–23
Matthew 28:16–20

READINGS FOR THE
SEVENTH SUNDAY OF EASTER
Acts 1;12–14
Psalm 27:1–4,7–8
1 Peter 4:13–16
John 17:1–11a

Monday

MAY 22

• ST. RITA OF CASCIA, RELIGIOUS •

"I have told you this so that you might have peace in me.
In the world you will have trouble,
but take courage, I have conquered the world."
—JOHN 16:32–33

Once in a while, for no apparent reason, I walk through the
day feeling bereft. It's a feeling of loss, as though a valuable
relationship has been taken from me. In today's Gospel Jesus
sheds light on that feeling of disconnection. "Behold, the
hour is coming . . . when each of you will be scattered to his
own home." When I feel this way, my usual distractions of
TV, sports news, or foraging the refrigerator offer no relief.
Jesus points to the real solution: "Have peace in me." Ah,
that's the relationship I've been missing. Now I can access
real peace—and I don't even have to remember my password.

Acts 19:1–8
Psalm 68:2–3ab,4–5acd,6–7ab
John 16:29–33

*"Now this is eternal life,
that they should know you, the only true God,
And the one whom you sent, Jesus Christ."*
—JOHN 17:3

For Jesus, to know someone is to see to the heart of the
person. Recall the times he would encounter someone in
need or distress. He would gaze on them and know the
nature of their distress. And in the encounter with this person
who would read their hearts with compassion and care,
seekers experienced new and abundant life. They were
healed not only of physical maladies but of soul-sickness as
well. Show up as who you are in prayer, and Jesus will share
God's life with you as well.

Acts 20:17–27
Psalm 68:10–11,20–21
John 17:1–11a

Wednesday

MAY 24

*"They do not belong to the world
any more than I belong to the world."*
—JOHN 17:14

A high-school theology teacher would frequently tell us clueless boys that we should be "in the world but not of the world." We assumed he was just trying to squelch our attempts at slightly illicit fun with the girls from the nearby Catholic girls' high school. But what he really meant was, "What do you stand for and who do you stand with?" He had been a missionary in a disastrously poor country, where he cherished the people he served. He returned to Chicago and was heartsick at the waste and exploitation that had become necessary to sustain what some call progress. He stood for justice and stood with his poor parishioners. We were left wondering. And that was his gift to us.

Acts 20:28–38
Psalm 68:29–30,33–35a,35bc–36ab
John 17:11b–19

⇒ 179 ⇐

Thursday

MAY 25

"I have given them the glory you gave me,
so that they may be one, as we are one,
I in them and you in me."
—JOHN 17:22–23

In the final chapters of John's Gospel Jesus engages in
lengthy theological discourses focused on the union he
shares with the Father and, by extension, with the disciples
and us. As I read today's reading, what came to me were the
words *Holy Communion*, and I thought, "The right gesture is
worth 10,000 words." Today, meditate on the deep meaning
of Jesus' simple actions: taking the bread and the wine,
consecrating it as his own body and blood, and sharing it
with those whom he so desired would become one—with
him, with the Father, with each other, and with all of us who
would follow in their faith steps.

Acts 22:30; 23:6–11
Psalm 16:1–2a and 5,7–8,9–10,11
John 17:20–26

As far as the east is from the west,
so far has he put our transgressions from us.
—PSALM 103:12

In the process of offering spiritual direction, I've seen how alive and powerful people's former transgressions can remain to them. I've seen that in myself as well—cringe moments when I recall a harm I have done, even though I've apologized, made amends, and been forgiven. Such inability to accept God's forgiveness reflects a lack of faith that keeps me from growing closer to God and others. Today, let us pray for the grace to fully receive forgiveness, and the grace to believe in our hearts that our transgressions have been taken away and sent packing—as far as the east is from the west.

Acts 25:13b–21
Psalm 103:1–2,11–12,19–20ab
John 21:15–19

*It is this disciple who testifies to these things
and has written them, and we know that his
testimony is true.*
—JOHN 21:24

The Easter season culminates tomorrow with Pentecost,
when the Holy Spirit descends on the apostles. But the day
before, the disciples were huddled together, still fearful, some
of them likely wondering if this was how it would end. We
know it was not the end because we have these Gospel
accounts, and the Epistles, and the catacombs, and the
churches, and the writings of the desert fathers and mothers,
as well as the lives of the saints, and the traditions handed
down from generation to generation, and the very fact that
people will be gathering tomorrow to celebrate the birthday
of the Church. And there is also you and me. Jesus Christ has
risen indeed, alleluia!

Acts 28:16–20,30–31
Psalm 11:4,5 and 7
John 21:20–25

MAY 28

• PENTECOST SUNDAY •

And suddenly there came from the sky
a noise like a strong driving wind,
and it filled the entire house in which they were.
—ACTS 2:2

The arrival of the Holy Spirit signals dramatic change, as reflected in today's many readings: Thunder on Mount Sinai, dry bones brought to life, trumpet blasts, all creation groaning, and formerly timid people proclaiming their faith boldly so that all can understand. The Holy Spirit has descended and the fearful are set free. Amen, alleluia!

VIGIL:
Genesis 11:1–9 or Exodus 19:3–8a,16–20b
or Ezekiel 37:1–4 or Joel 3:1–5
Psalm 104:1–2,24,35,27–28,29,30
Romans 8:22–27
John 7:37–39

EXTENDED VIGIL:
Genesis 11:1–9
Exodus 19:3–8a,16–20b

Ezekiel 37:1–14
Joel 3:1–5
Romans 8:22–27
John 7:37–39

DAY:
Acts 2:1–11
Psalm 104:1,24,29–30,31,34
1 Corinthians 12:3b–7,12–13
John 20:19–23

Monday

MAY 29

• FEAST OF THE BLESSED VIRGIN MARY, MOTHER OF THE CHURCH •

When Jesus saw his mother and the disciple there whom he loved,
he said to his mother, "Woman, behold, your son."
Then he said to the disciple,
"Behold, your mother."
And from that hour the disciple took her into his home.
—JOHN 19:25–26

Once again, Jesus implores those he loves to "behold." It is an invitation from the cross to see as he sees, in this case the disciple he loves and the mother who bore him. Mary, Mother of the Church, looks upon us all with love and desire for our good. Let us emulate Saint John and welcome Mary into the home of our hearts.

Genesis 3:9–15, 20 or Acts 1:12–14
Psalm 87:1–2, 3 and 5, 6–7
John 19:25–34

In a generous spirit pay homage to the LORD,
be not sparing of freewill gifts.
—SIRACH 35:10

The prophets were often most concerned about right
relationships, how we relate to God and to others. As Sirach
did in today's first reading, they warned that God is not
pleased with empty, showy, self-aggrandizing gestures.
Sirach says the sacrifices we are called to make are not burnt
offerings but rather our freely taken actions of charity,
justice, generosity, and joy. He says we should not arrive in
prayer empty-handed but with a day's worth of actions taken
for others, all done gratefully with a generous and cheerful
spirit. If we get our relationships right with God and others,
our best behavior will follow.

Sirach 35:1–12
Psalm 50:5–6,7–8,14 and 23
Mark 10:28–31

MAY 31

*"Blessed are you, O Virgin Mary, who believed
that what was spoken to you by the Lord would be fulfilled."*
—LUKE 1:45

Women gather for mutual support. Today we celebrate the visitation of Mary to her cousin Elizabeth, mother to John the Baptist. As often happens when women gather, Elizabeth offered words of support to Mary, pointing out where her dear friend and cousin exemplified true faith. We need faith to face life's many uncertainties, and Mary and Elizabeth faced many difficult moments due to how their sons were perceived and treated in the world. Faith doesn't mean we won't face hardships; it means that we will not face them alone. God's presence will always be there—sometimes mediated by a cousin, a best friend, or even a stranger.

Zephaniah 3:14–18a or Romans 12:9–16
Isaiah 12:2–3,4bcd,5–6
Luke 1:39–56

JUNE 1

• ST. JUSTIN, MARTYR •

"Take courage; get up, Jesus is calling you."
He threw aside his cloak, sprang up, and came to Jesus.
Jesus said to him in reply "What do you want me to
do for you?"
The blind man replied to him, "Master, I want to see."
—MARK 10:49–51

I can go a long time in my day before paying any attention to my relationship with Jesus. And yet Jesus stands nearby asking, "What do you want me to do for you?" Usually my response is, "I want to see my way out of a difficult situation or unhelpful mood I could have avoided if I'd asked you for help first thing this morning." Take courage. Jesus awaits and has a question for you.

Sirach 42:15–25
Psalm 33:2–3,4–5,6–7,8–9
Mark 10:46–52

Friday

JUNE 2

• ST. MARCELLINUS AND ST. PETER, MARTYRS •

The Lord takes delight in his people.
—PSALM 149:4

Time to check in on your unconscious perception of God. If you hear the phrase, "God is watching you," what comes to mind? Are you picturing a stern judge? A nosy neighbor? A person looking upon you with delight? As for me, I have had to cultivate that last scenario through practice and trust. And yet, when I can sense God looking at me with delight, it changes everything. It brings out the best in me and increases my desire to share that delight with others. Let the words of the psalm sink into your heart.

Sirach 44:1,9–13
Psalm 149:1b–2,3–4,5–6a and 9b
Mark 11:11–26

The chief priests, the scribes, and the elders
approached him and said to him,
"By what authority are you doing these things?"
—MARK 1:27–28

The chief priests, scribes, and elders were hoping to trap
Jesus. Jesus was trying to invite them to abundant life. They
put a question to Jesus that was designed to make him look
bad. He decided instead to hold a mirror up to them by
asking a question that would reveal their true duplicity. We
can't enter the kingdom of God through arrogance and lies.
If we want to know the truth about Jesus, we must first be
willing to know the truth about ourselves.

Sirach 51:12cd–20
Psalm 19:8,9,10,11
Mark 11:27–33

Sunday

JUNE 4

• THE MOST HOLY TRINITY •

Moses at once bowed down to the ground in worship.
Then he said, "If I find favor with you, O LORD,
do come along in our company.
This is indeed a stiff-necked people;
yet pardon our wickedness and sins,
and receive us as your own."
—EXODUS 34:8–9

This passage signals a turning point in the relationship between God and his people. Yahweh had rescued the people from slavery in Egypt. Now, Moses was inviting him to "come along in our company" as they wandered in the desert on their way to the Promised Land. We may also experience turning points in our relationship with God at which we don't just look for help in times of crisis but invite him, as we wander our own deserts, to "come along in our company" and "receive us as your own."

Exodus 34:4b–6,8–9
Daniel 3:52,53,54,55,56 (52b)
2 Corinthians 13:11–13
John 3:16–18

Monday

JUNE 5

• ST. BONIFACE, BISHOP AND MARTYR •

The neighbors mocked me, saying to one another:
"He is still not afraid!
Once before he was hunted down for execution
because of this very thing;
yet now that he has scarcely escaped,
here he is again burying the dead!"
—TOBIT 2:8

Tobit, exiled in Nineveh, was scorned as a foreigner. Yet he was faithful and wise and caring. When a fellow Jew was murdered and left dead in the street, Tobit sent his son to retrieve the body so they could, at great risk to themselves, give their compatriot a proper burial. Honoring the dead continues to be a moral imperative. Today, honor someone important in your life who has died, by reaching out to someone who is still mourning their loss.

Tobit 1:3; 2:1a–8
Psalm 112:1b–2,3b–4,5–6
Mark 12:1–12

Tuesday

JUNE 6

• ST. NORBERT, BISHOP •

"Repay to Caesar what belongs to Caesar
and to God what belongs to God."
—MARK 12:17

Today's Gospel reading features one of Jesus' most famous
statements, turning the tables on the Pharisees' false choice
of whether to show allegiance to Caesar or to God. His
response puts the responsibility back on them to decide what
belongs to Caesar and what belongs to God. Centuries later,
St. Ignatius of Loyola stated his position in this famous
prayer: "Take, Lord, and receive all my liberty, my memory,
my understanding, and my entire will, all I have and call my
own. You have given all to me. To you, Lord, I return it.
Everything is yours; do with it what you will. Give me only
your love and your grace, that is enough for me."

Tobit 2:9–14
Psalm 112:1–2,7–8,9
Mark 12:13–17

To you, O Lord, I lift my soul.
—PSALM 25:1

How do you pray? I suspect that as long as we're sincere, there's no wrong way to pray. I've come to believe that prayer is both less than what I first thought it should be, and also more. That is, prayer now typically involves fewer words and more presence. But don't take it from me: *The Catechism of the Catholic Church* says, "Prayer is the raising of one's mind and heart to God" (CCC 2590), which describes a kind of yearning expressed with or without words. And it's important to know also that God is the one who initiates the experience: "God tirelessly calls each person to a mysterious encounter with himself." (CCC 2591). So don't get hung up on how to define prayer; just answer God's call to encounter, and lift up your soul.

Tobit 3:1–11a,16–17a
Psalm 25:2–3,4–5ab,6 and 7bc,8–9
Mark 12:18–27

Thursday

JUNE 8

*"And to love him with all your heart,
with all your understanding,
with all your strength,
and to love your neighbor as yourself
is worth more than all burnt offerings and sacrifices."*
—MARK 12:33

Humans can sometimes reduce religious practice to a set of rules and actions disconnected from what is in our hearts. We go through the motions because it's the right thing to do, which is not bad. Yet there's so much more to the Good News than dutiful obedience. There's love, which is not a duty but a total transformation of the heart, understanding, strength, and self. Pray today, "God, help me to know you, so that I may love you and serve you in everyone I meet."

Tobit 6:10–11; 7:1bcde,9–17; 8:4–9a
Psalm 128:1–2,3,4–5
Mark 12:28–34

Friday

JUNE 9

*When Tobit saw his son, he threw his arms around
him and wept.
He exclaimed, "I can see you, son, the light of my eyes!"*
—TOBIT 11:13–14

The story of Tobit is a charming account of a Job-like character who was faithful to God and generous to others. In his old age, he was beset by physical and spiritual challenges. He sent his son Tobiah on a perilous journey to secure help for the family. Along the way, Tobiah encountered a helper and guide, Raphael, who appeared as a man but who is later revealed to be an archangel. The story reminds me of the angels I've encountered, helpful strangers who appeared in my life at times of distress, danger, or deep need. God has many ways to help us if only we are open to receive them.

Tobit 11:5–17
Psalm 146:1b–2,6c–7,8–9a,9bc–10
Mark 12:35–37

Many rich people put in large sums.
A poor widow also came and put in two small coins
worth a few cents.
Calling his disciples to himself, he said to them,
"Amen, I say to you, this poor widow put in more
than all the other contributor the treasury."
—MARK 12:41–43

As I was praying with today's Gospel, an unsettling question came to mind: "How would I react if Jesus was talking about sharing time rather than money?" The point of the Gospel extends beyond money to how we choose to use all the resources at our disposal—including time, attention, and care. Today, I'll pray for the grace to see what I may be secretly withholding—even from myself—and how I can be more trusting, like the widow who gave her all.

Tobit 12:1,5–15,20
Tobit 13:2,6efgh,7,8
Mark 12:38–44

Sunday

JUNE 11

[Jesus said,] "I am the living bread that came down from heaven;
whoever eats this bread will live forever."
—JOHN 6:51

I love watching people come up to receive communion. They
sometimes reveal so much: their deep desire, their worries
and cares, their joyful anticipation, a level of vulnerability
you rarely see in daily life. The Eucharist is where God's
overwhelming love meets our great longing, and in that Holy
Communion we truly become the Body of Christ. It's the
culmination of all Jesus' teaching, all Christ's desire since
before the dawn of time. Don't miss it!

Deuteronomy 8:2–3,14b–16a
Psalm 147:12–13,14–15,19–20 (12)
1 Corinthians 10:16–17
John 6:51–58

When Jesus saw the crowds, he went up the mountain,
and after he had sat down, his disciples came to him.
He began to teach them, saying:
"Blessed are the poor in spirit."
—MATTHEW 5:2–3

Jesus saw the crowds. He didn't just glance at them, he looked deeply, as was his way, and he saw they were like sheep without a shepherd. He decided that he would not just see them but he would also let them see what he sees, so they might love what he loves. From the mount, a place of Divine authority, Jesus gave them the Beatitudes, which are ways of being: Be merciful. Be clean of heart. Be just . . . and you will know God, see God, and join God in healing the world. The Beatitudes are worth studying and contemplating. They open the gate to the kingdom of Heaven.

2 Corinthians 1:1–7
Psalm 34:2–3,4–5,6–7,8–9
Matthew 5:1–12

Tuesday

JUNE 13

"Just so, your light must shine before others,
that they may see your good deeds
and glorify your heavenly Father."
—MATTHEW 5:16

Do you know your own light? Are you aware of the splinter of brilliance within you that is of God and yet uniquely you? In this world brimming with so many brands and flavors of darkness, it can make us uncertain when even trying to recognize the inner light of Christ we are endowed with. But it's there. And it's necessary that you let it shine so that the darkness of chaos, violence, and oppression can be illuminated and overcome. It can be difficult to trust our own light, or even believe our light has any meaning and purpose outside ourselves. Jesus knew otherwise. Remember, one small candle will illuminate an otherwise totally dark room.

2 Corinthians 1:18–22
Psalm 119:129,130,131,132,133,135
Matthew 5:13–16

Our qualification comes from God,
who has indeed qualified us as ministers
of a new covenant.
—2 CORINTHIANS 3:5–6

I was shaking as I entered the classroom on my first day of teaching religion to high-school juniors and seniors. It didn't go well. Down in the teacher's lounge, a veteran teacher who was respected by her students gave me sage advice: Prepare well, speak from your heart with confidence, trust the outcome to the Holy Spirit. St. Paul says it is God who qualifies us and gives us the confidence to speak about faith. That's true for teachers, catechists, parents, and grandparents. A few years ago, I attended a reunion of those students I'd taught that first year. Judging by how well they turned out in life and in faith, the Holy Spirit did a very fine job.

2 Corinthians 3:4–11
Psalm 99:5,6,7,8,9
Matthew 5:17–19

JUNE 15

Therefore, if you bring your gift to the altar,
and there recall that your brother
has anything against you,
leave your gift there at the altar,
go first and be reconciled with your brother,
and then come and offer your gift.
—MATTHEW 5:23–24

Blessed are the single-hearted. Blessed are they whose insides match the outsides of their lives, who are the same person 24/7. Unfortunately, we often fall short of that goal. Our ability to rationalize and self-defend creates blind spots where we fail to see the discrepancies between our self-image and the reality underlying it. Jesus knows we have this problem and shows what to do to resolve it: clean up your side of the street, then walk whole-heartedly to the altar.

2 Corinthians 3:15—4:1,3–6
Psalm 85:9ab and 10,11–12,13–14
Matthew 5:20–26

Friday

JUNE 16

• THE SACRED HEART OF JESUS •

Beloved, if God so loved us,
we must also love one another.
—1 JOHN 4:11

Today we celebrate the feast of the Sacred Heart of Jesus,
tomorrow, the feast of the Immaculate Heart of Mary. We
might dismiss these feasts as flowery and overly sweet. But
these hearts bear wounds: Jesus' heart is scourged with
thorns. Mary's heart is pierced by a sword. These are symbols
of what they carried in their hearts—wounds endured
willingly out of compassion for the suffering of others.
Religiously, the heart symbolizes the defining essence of the
person. Both Jesus and his blessed mother led lives in which
their hearts were open, vulnerable, and shining beacons
reflecting the Father's love. What's in your heart today?

Deuteronomy 7:6–11
Psalm 103:1–2,3–4,6–7,8,10 (see 17)
1 John 4:7–16
Matthew 11:25–30

So whoever is in Christ is a new creation.
—2 CORINTHIANS 5:17

Believers tell stories about Jesus and the saints that, while not verifiably true, capture and convey a truth about the person. Have you heard this one about St. Teresa of Avila? One day the devil appeared to her disguised as Christ. Teresa wasn't fooled and sent him away. As he left, the devil asked, "How did you know?" Teresa answered, "Christ has wounds! You didn't have any." On this feast of the Immaculate Heart of Mary, it's good to ponder Jesus' wounds and how they were gained *for* us; and Mary's wounds that were gained *as* one of us. We all acquire wounds over a lifetime, and when we unite them with the wounds of Christ, as Mary did as she stood at the foot of the Cross, our own wounds become sacred wounds.

2 Corinthians 5:14–21
Psalm 103:1–2,3–4,9–10,11–12
Luke 2:41–51

Sunday

JUNE 18

Know that the LORD is God;
he made us, his we are,
his people, the flock he tends.
—PSALM 100:3

Sometimes, at the end of a crazy day, I feel as though I've just gotten off a tilt-a-whirl ride that went on too long. My wife will find me shaking my head and mumbling, "I don't know anything." So, I slow down, breathe deeply, and take note of what I do know, beginning with a litany of my blessings (the love of my wife and family, my delightful friends, the people I encountered that day who brought light into my life, etc.). Eventually I arrive at the foundational belief on which all others rest: "I know that God loves me and cares for me, and I love God." And then I can breathe easier, knowing I stand on solid, and sacred, ground.

Exodus 19:2–6a
Psalm 100:1–2,3,5 (3c)
Romans 5:6–11
Matthew 9:36—10:8

[Jesus said,] "You have heard that it was said,
An eye for an eye and a tooth for a tooth.
But I say to you, offer no resistance to one who is evil."
—MATTHEW 5:38–39

The urge for retaliation seems hardwired into the human mind and nervous system. That's why Jesus' call to nonviolent response is rarely achieved by willpower alone, especially when the wounds are old and deeply seared into our memory. St. Ignatius, a hotheaded soldier who suffered a stinging defeat, found a way beyond retaliation. He prayed, "Take Lord, receive all my liberty, my memory, my understanding, my entire will . . ." Let's focus on memory. Our memories carry not only events but also energy. Sometimes those memories need to be healed. Turn your hurtful memories over to God's care, and help prevent the world from becoming blind and toothless.

2 Corinthians 6:1–10
Psalm 98:1,2b,3ab,3cd–4
Matthew 5:38–42

JUNE 20

[Jesus said,] "You have heard that it was said,
You shall love your neighbor and hate your enemy.
But I say to you, love your enemies,
and pray for those who persecute you."
—MATTHEW 5:43–44

This is one of Jesus' clearest directives, and also one of the hardest to achieve. Fear of others (those we see as our enemies) closes off our hearts. Add hate to the mix and our hearts become hardened, leaving little if any room for love. So what can we do? Jesus offers a good first step: pray for them. Really. You don't have to like it. You don't (at first) even need to mean it. But attempt to pray for those you resent, loathe, or out-and-out hate. If you find yourself unwilling, begin by praying for the willingness to be willing. A wise friend tells me, if you do your 1 percent, God will manage the other 99 percent. You just have to sincerely try.

2 Corinthians 8:1–9
Psalm 146:2,5–6ab,6c–7,8–9a
Matthew 5:43–48

Wednesday
JUNE 21
• ST. ALOYSIUS GONZAGA, RELIGIOUS •

"And your Father who sees what is hidden
will repay you."
—MATTHEW 6:18

Faith is an inside job. Matthew in particular harps on the need to interiorize what Jesus preaches and make it a natural part of who we have become. Jesus had lost patience with the self-proclaimed holy people around him who blew trumpets before handing over their donations or who prayed loudly and obviously on street corners, or who put on the grunge look during times of fasting—just because. We all want to be good. Some settle for appearing good. But the posers miss out on the true reward awaiting those who know that goodness flows from God, not from deceptive optics.

2 Corinthians 9:6–11
Psalm 112:1bc–2,3–4,9
Matthew 6:1–6,16–18

• ST. PAULINUS OF NOLA, BISHOP • ST. JOHN FISHER, BISHOP, AND ST. THOMAS MORE, MARTYRS •

[Jesus said,] "This is how you are to pray:
Our Father, who art in heaven,
hallowed be thy name,
thy kingdom come,
thy will be done,
on earth as it is in heaven.
Give us this day our daily bread;
and forgive us our trespasses,
as we forgive those who trespass against us;
and lead us not into temptation,
but deliver us from evil."
—MATTHEW 6:9–13

Time out. Slow down. Read the first line out loud and pause. Give it a good pause. Then move on to the next. Read it aloud a few times until its familiarity has worn off. Continue through the whole prayer, slowly, thoughtfully, with fresh eyes and fresh ears. Let it sink in. Stay awake! This is the prayer that Jesus gave us.

2 Corinthians 11:1–11
Psalm 111:1b–2,3–4,7–8
Matthew 6:7–15

Friday

JUNE 23

"Do not store up for yourselves treasures on earth,
where moth and decay destroy, and thieves
break in and steal. . . .
For where your treasure is, there also will your heart be."
—MATTHEW 6:19–21

These days Jesus might say, "Do not acquire treasures for
which you'll have to rent remote storage units and when you
die your heirs will immediately call 1-800-Got-Junk."
Matthew's view of Jesus focuses more on the interior as
opposed to the exterior of life. Rather than "What's in your
wallet?" he'd be asking "What's in your heart?" That's why so
much of Christian spirituality is about detaching from the
things of the world and embracing the love of God, which is
the only thing that truly satisfies, freeing us to live graciously
in the world of objects and possessions.

2 Corinthians 11:18,21–30
Psalm 34:2–3,4–5,6–7
Matthew 6:19–23

JUNE 24

• THE NATIVITY OF ST. JOHN THE BAPTIST •

To whomever I send you, you shall go;
whatever I command you, you shall speak.
Have no fear before them,
because I am with you to deliver you, says the LORD.
—JEREMIAH 1:7–8

Mark Twain reportedly said, "I have known many troubles in my life, most of which never happened." I know the feeling. Worrying-in-advance syndrome. Jeremiah worried too. He cried to the Lord, "I know not how to speak; I am too young." He was worried that the people God was sending him to would ignore him—or worse. God assured him, as he assures us, "Have no fear. I am with you." We get a lot of practice worrying. We need to also practice letting go of fear and trusting instead. Trust not that everything will go perfectly but that God is with you no matter what.

VIGIL:	DAY:
Jeremiah 1:4–10	Isaiah 49:1–6
Psalm 71:1–2,3–4a,5–6ab,15ab and 17	Psalm 139:1b–3,13–14ab,14c–15
1 Peter 1:8–12	Acts 13:22–26
Luke 1:5–17	Luke 1:57–66,80

For your sake I bear insult,
and shame covers my face.
—PSALM 69:8

People who graciously bear insults mystify me. In hoping to learn from today's psalm I discovered that the psalmist prayed to be rescued "from the mire." "Don't let me sink," he cried. Yep, that pretty much captures how it feels to be insulted. He begs the Lord, "Do not hide your face from your servant." Ahh, the answer is to keep my eyes on the face of God, because God sees all and heals all. When I try to hide what I'm feeling from God and trustworthy others, the more I sink in the mire of my ego. God, who sees me, wants to free me and lift me up to solid ground, knowing that nothing can separate me from his love and high regard.

Jeremiah 20:10–13
Psalm 69:8–10,14,17,33–35 (14c)
Romans 5:12–15
Matthew 10:26–33

*"Why do you notice the splinter in your brother's eye,
but do not perceive the wooden beam
in your own eye?"*
—MATTHEW 7:3

In today's Gospel Jesus addresses a great human pastime: judging others. Jesus recognizes the dynamic at work—we judge others to avoid judging ourselves. In fact, we project onto others that which we fear might be true of ourselves.

That's not the way to enter the reign of God, a state of communion, solidarity, and mutual forgiveness. What can we do instead of judging? Cut people some slack! Receive reality graciously, knowing that with God's grace, everything, including our own faults and foibles, can be redeemed.

Genesis 12:1–9
Psalm 33:12–13,18–19,20 and 22
Matthew 7:1–5

JUNE 27

• ST. CYRIL OF ALEXANDRIA, BISHOP AND DOCTOR OF THE CHURCH •

Who shall live on your holy mountain, O LORD?
He who walks blamelessly and does justice;
who thinks the truth in his heart
and slanders not with his tongue.
—PSALM 15:1B–3

The line extoling the person "who thinks the truth in his [or her] heart" is a rich statement, one worth some reflection. It brings to mind how tempted I can be to rationalize my actions, shade the truth to make me feel better about myself, or bend a story to put me in a better light, and so on. Yet, when I read the lives of saints, I am inspired by how able they were to see themselves plain, with great humility and no self-deception. It calls to mind a prayer of Pope John Paul I: "Lord, take me as I am, with my faults and with my sins, but make me become as you wish."

Genesis 13:2,5–18
Psalm 15:2–3a,3bc–4ab,5
Matthew 7:6,12–14

JUNE 28

*[Jesus said,] "Beware of false prophets, who come to you
in sheep's clothing,
but underneath are ravenous wolves."*
—MATTHEW 7:15

People get taken in by false prophets when they are feeling
powerless, afraid, or out of control in a changing world.
They look for certainty without ambiguity, and that's where
the false prophet finds his or her way in, by telling people
what they want to hear. By their fruits you shall know them.
Here are three characteristics I've noticed in modern false
prophets: They offer simplistic answers to complex
questions; they seek to accumulate personal power while
disempowering others; they are motivated (and motivate
others) by fear rather than love.

Genesis 15:1–12,17–18
Psalm 105:1–2,3–4,6–7,8–9
Matthew 7:15–20

JUNE 29

• ST. PETER AND ST. PAUL, APOSTLES •

Suddenly, the angel of the Lord stood by him,
and a light shone in the cell.
He tapped Peter on the side and awakened him, saying,
"Get up quickly."
The chains fell from his wrists.
—ACTS 12:7

I have a postcard on my desk, purchased in Rome while visiting St. Peter in Chains Basilica. The basilica houses two sets of chains, now fused together. They each shackled St. Peter while in prison, once early on in Jerusalem and the other time, near the end, in Rome's Mamertine Prison, where St. Paul had also been held. On this feast of Sts. Peter and Paul, the postcard reminds me that faith has its price—and that I should faithfully pay my daily share, which has been, "til now, far less than what was asked of Peter, Paul, and countless other Christians."

VIGIL:	DAY:
Acts 3:1–10	Acts 12:1–11
Psalm 19:2–3,4–5	Psalm 34:2–3,4–5,6–7,8–9
Galatians 1:11–20	2 Timothy 4:6–8,17–18
John 21:15–19	Matthew 16:13–19

When Jesus came down from the mountain,
great crowds followed him.
And then a leper approached, did him homage, and said,
"Lord, if you wish, you can make me clean."
—MATTHEW 8:1–2

Do you spend time praying before you face a difficult meeting? Jesus did. The Gospels frequently tell of Jesus spending time communing with the Father in prayer prior to preaching, healing, or casting out demons. How about you? Do you spend intentional time with the Father before a major task or encounter, whether you expect it to be easy-breezy or confrontational? Five minutes can be enough if you approach God with an open heart. And you don't even need to schedule an appointment.

Genesis 17:1,9–10,15–22
Psalm 128:1–2,3,4–5
Matthew 8:1–4

Saturday
JULY 1
• ST. JUNÍPERO SERRA, PRIEST •

*[Mary said,] "My soul proclaims the greatness of the Lord,
my spirit rejoices in God my Savior."*
—LUKE 1:46

We're at the halfway point on the calendar, a good time to take stock of everything God has done for us in the past six or seven months. On January 1 we make a list of resolutions. How about on July 1 we create a new habit of making a daily gratitude list? Keep it simple. On a slip of paper write a descending list from 1 to 10. Ask the Holy Spirit for guidance and a good memory, and start listing people, places, and things you are grateful for from the past twenty-four hours. Some will make the list each day. How great is that! But dig deep and make sure at least a few new things make the cut each day. Your spirit will rejoice.

Genesis 18:1–15
Luke 1:46–47,48–49,50 and 53,54–55
Matthew 8:5–17

Sunday

JULY 2

• THIRTEENTH SUNDAY IN ORDINARY TIME •

*[Jesus said,] "Whoever finds his life will lose it,
and whoever loses his life for my sake will find it."*
—MATTHEW 10:39

You need to die before you die. Huh? Yes, you have to die in this lifetime (in some significant way) before you can enter the kingdom of heaven. Those of you who tend to take things literally, I beg you to take a breath or two. There are times when being literal pays off. But not when you encounter paradox. Nobel Prize-winning physicist Niels Bohr wrote, "The opposite of a true statement is a false statement, but the opposite of a profound truth can be another profound truth." The spiritual practice for handling a paradox is to spend time with the two conflicting profound truths. Befriend them. Ask God to help you embrace both sides of the paradox. And breathe!

2 Kings 4:8–11,14–16a
Psalm 89:2–3,16–17,18–19 (2a)
Romans 6:3–4,8–11
Matthew 10:37–42

Monday

JULY 3

• ST. THOMAS, APOSTLE •

But Thomas said to them,
"Unless I see the mark of the nails in his hands
and put my finger into the nailmarks
and put my hand into his side, I will not believe."
—JOHN 20:25

As a kid named Thomas, I was deeply disappointed in Thomas the apostle. In my earnest desire to appear holy, it bothered me to be associated with "Doubting Thomas," the apostle who questioned Jesus's resurrection. Doubting seemed such a betrayal. But I grew up and painfully came to realize the value of doubting as a way of deepening my faith. Doubting helps clarify. It gives you "skin in the game." But remember this: Doubts can erode your confidence. Allow yourself to have at least as much faith in your faith as you do in your doubts.

Ephesians 2:19–22
Psalm 117:1bc,2
John 20:24–29

⇒ 219 ⇐

Tuesday

JULY 4

• INDEPENDENCE DAY •

*But Lot's wife looked back, and she was turned
into a pillar of salt.*
—GENESIS 19:26

Pretty harsh punishment, eh? Just one quick peek at the place
where she lived, loved, and gave birth to her children, and
now she's a pillar of salt? Where's the spiritual sense in that?
It helps to understand that Lot and his wife were being
guided away from the unsavory Sodom and Gomorrah just
before its destruction, to a place of safety where a better
future could unfold. Sometimes we sabotage ourselves,
making bold commitments to a better way of living and
yet . . . we look back longingly to our old unhealthy ways,
and the look becomes a turn, and the bright new future
becomes our dreary old past once again. As I once read on a
bumper sticker, "When you're going through hell, don't stop!"

Genesis 19:15–29
Psalm 26:2–3,9–10,11–12
Matthew 8:23–27

⇉ 220 ⇇

Wednesday
JULY 5

• ST. ELIZABETH OF PORTUGAL • ST. ANTHONY MARY ZACCARIA, PRIEST •

When the poor one cried out, the LORD heard,
and from all his distress he saved him.
The angel of the LORD encamps
around those who fear him, and delivers them.
—PSALM 34:7–8

How are we to understand "fear" of the Lord? I suspect we
don't have an adequate word in English to express all that is
encompassed in that phrase, but I deeply believe that one
shade of meaning has to be reverence. Another that comes to
mind is profound respect for One who is someone to be
reckoned with. Jesus was clear that we are not to be terrified
of God, especially if it blocks our drawing closer to God. But
for our own good and the good of the world, God is not to
be ignored. To use playwright Arthur Miller's powerful words
in an entirely different context, "Attention must be paid."

Genesis 21:5,8–20a
Psalm 34:7–8,10–11,12–13
Matthew 8:28–34

⇒ 221 ⇐

Thursday

JULY 6

• ST. MARIA GORETTI, VIRGIN AND MARTYR •

*Thereupon Abraham took the wood
for the burnt offering
and laid it on his son Isaac's shoulders.*
—GENESIS 22:6

I believe that it's worth struggling sincerely with a core passage of Scripture, even when the struggle remains unresolved. My struggle with putting myself in Abraham's shoes is twofold: to acquiesce to God's instruction to sacrifice my child's life would be a betrayal of my vocation as father and grandfather, and it would be telling a lie to my child about the God I've come to know and love, in effect, laying it on his or her shoulders. As a spiritual director I've seen the lasting effects of having been given as a child a faulty image of God. Someday I might be able to see beyond these stumbling blocks. But for now, I can recommit to my vocation as dad and grandpa.

Genesis 22:1b–19
Psalm 115:1–2,3–4,5–6,8–9
Matthew 9:1–8

*The Pharisees saw this and said to his disciples,
"Why does your teacher eat with tax collectors
and sinners?"*
—MATTHEW 9:13

Mercy is what moved Jesus to pursue Matthew. Matthew was a local tax collector, someone known for corruption and dishonesty. But Jesus saw more in Matthew than what he may have done or failed to do. He saw a man who was ready to change his ways, a man whose future could be far greater than his past. And that's all Jesus needed to make him willing to risk the ritual impurity of eating with sinners to find another lost sheep. What is the something more that Jesus sees in you? Can you welcome him into your mess to find out more?

Genesis 23:1–4,19; 24:1–8,62–67
Psalm 106:1b–2. 3–4a, 4b–5
Matthew 9:9–13

[Isaac said,] "May God give to you
of the dew of the heavens
And of the fertility of the earth
abundance of grain and wine."
—GENESIS 27:28

Today seems like a good time to back away from the clashes
between Jesus and the scribes and Pharisees and dwell for a
while on this lovely blessing that Isaac offered to his son
Jacob. Clearly, God, from whom all blessings flow, desires
good things for us as well. Today, let nature speak to you and
bless you in ways that gladden your heart.

Genesis 27:1–5,15–29
Psalm 135:1b–2,3–4,5–6
Matthew 9:14–17

Sunday

JULY 9

• FOURTEENTH SUNDAY IN ORDINARY TIME •

*[Jesus said,] "Come to me all you who labor and are burdened
and I will give you rest.
Take my yoke upon you and learn from me,
for I am meek and humble of heart."*
—MATTHEW 11:28–29

How is anyone to find rest in this overworked, overworried world? Jesus says, "Learn from me," and then he shows the way, saying, "for I am meek and humble of heart." Hmmm, meek and humble? How can that help? Meekness grounds us in God, allowing us to trust in God's saving grace. Meekness, the opposite of arrogance, is quietly persistent and brave.

Humility lets us admit we have a role to play but the outcome is not up to us. There is a God, and, fortunately, it is not me. I can turn off the worry switch and meekly and humbly put all my worries in God's hands.

Zechariah 9:9–10
Psalm 145:1–2,8–9,10–11,13–14
Romans 8:9,11–13
Matthew 11:25–30

When Jacob awoke from his sleep, he exclaimed,
"Truly, the LORD is in this spot, although
I did not know it!"
—GENESIS 28:16

"Nothing externally changed, but everything changed that day." That's a quote from a young friend who went on a retreat, had an encounter with God, and was amazed that God had always been that close. Have you had an experience like that? Such encounters serve a great purpose. They open a door that needs to be opened. And they can remind us, when the initial amazement fades, of something we now know in our flesh—that God longs to be with us and always welcomes our return. Savoring memories like that is a form of prayer. Try it again today.

Genesis 28:10–22a
Psalm 91:1–2,3–4,14–15ab
Matthew 9:18–26

Hearken to my prayer from lips without deceit.
—PSALM 17:1

In his book *Praying the Truth*, the late William Barry, SJ, shared an insight that came during prayer. "One day God seemed to be telling me, 'Most of the time when you ask me what I want from you, you're looking for something to do for me. I don't want you to do anything for me; I want you to be my friend, to let me reveal myself to you and for you to reveal yourself to me. The things-to-do will take care of themselves.'" "We may feel that God already knows everything about me," Barry says. "It's not about the information God might have; it's about whether you will trust God enough to say what is on your heart and mind and wait for a response." Be an honest-to-God believer.

Genesis 32:23–33
Psalm 17:1b,2–3,6–7ab,8b and 15
Matthew 9:32–38

JULY 12

Sing to him a new song;
pluck the strings skillfully, with shouts of gladness.
—PSALM 33:3

At a Mass celebrating the Viatorian priests who founded and
shepherded our parish 133 years prior, I found myself
perturbed. Our parish was merging with another, and new
leadership had been assigned. I was hoping we'd sing some of
my favorite hymns. But the choir from the 12:30
Spanish-language Mass was providing the music, not the crew
from my usual 8:30 Mass. I was disappointed because it wasn't
what I expected. But then the drummers started a beat and
guitarists started strumming, and people started clapping
along, and soon I was singing a new song and grateful that the
Viatorians had been so inclusive and prepared us all not just for
a new song but for a new day—one that the Lord had made.

Genesis 41:55–57; 42:5–7a,17–24a
Psalm 33:2–3,10–11,18–19
Matthew 10:1–7

[Jesus said,] "As you go, make this proclamation:
'The Kingdom of heaven is at hand.'
Cure the sick, raise the dead,
cleanse the lepers, drive out demons.
Without cost you have received; without cost
you are to give."
—MATTHEW 10:7–8

A friend of mine taught me a lesson about focusing attention. My family needed to get rid of "stuff" from our basement and garage, so we had a garage sale. I put up a decent-sized sign that read "Garage Sale." My friend came by to see how things were going, shook his head, and made a jumbo sign that said GARAGE SALE NOW!!! The number of browsers more than tripled. Maybe we should have signs in our homes reminding us THE KINGDOM OF HEAVEN STARTS NOW!!! The truth is, it is always now.

Genesis 44:18–21,23b–29; 45:1–5
Psalm 105:16–17,18–19,20–21
Matthew 10:7–15

Friday

JULY 14

• ST. KATERI TEKAKWITHA, VIRGIN •

Jesus said to his Apostles:
"Behold, I am sending you like sheep
in the midst of wolves;
so be shrewd as serpents and simple as doves."
—MATTHEW 10:16

Jesus's words of warning to the apostles are clever and also challenging to carry out. "Be shrewd as serpents and simple as doves" offers a paradoxical statement that believers still wrestle with today. We're to be shrewd as he was when the scribes and Pharisees tried to trick him into blasphemous statements. And we're to be softhearted as doves when sinners and outcasts show the slightest signs of repentance and acceptance of faith. Have you struggled with this in your life lately? Remember, Jesus sent the Holy Spirit, who helps us know when to bring on the serpent and when to reach for the dove.

Genesis 46:1–7,28–30
Psalm 37:3–4,18–19,27–28,39–40
Matthew 10:16–23

⇒ 230 ⇐

• ST. BONAVENTURE, BISHOP AND DOCTOR OF THE CHURCH •

But Joseph replied to [his brothers]:
"Have no fear. Can I take the place of God?
Even though you meant harm to me,
God meant it for good,
to achieve his present end, the survival
of many people."
—GENESIS 50:19–20

What's the hardest thing you've had to forgive? Consider Joseph, son of Jacob, whose eleven jealous brothers sold him into slavery in Egypt. Joseph grew to be the governor, responsible for feeding countless people during a widespread famine. His brothers came begging for help, not recognizing the official as the brother they had betrayed. Joseph showed magnanimity in forgiving his brothers and promising to care for their families. Rather than focusing on the betrayal, Joseph focused on what was made possible—the use of his gifts to help God achieve great things.

Genesis 49:29–32; 50:15–26a
Psalm 105:1–2,3–4,6–7
Matthew 10:24–33

JULY 16

• FIFTEENTH SUNDAY IN ORDINARY TIME •

[Jesus said,] "Some fell on rocky ground, where it had little soil.
It sprang up at once because the soil was not deep,
and when the sun rose it was scorched,
and it withered for lack of roots."
—MATTHEW 13:5–6

Sometimes I feel like a rocky-ground Christian. I respond to an insightful homily or retreat experience with great enthusiasm and many resolutions, but soon the excitement fades, and I suffer spiritual amnesia. Real growth comes from small choices repeated faithfully over time. What I do today matters. And tomorrow, and the next day, and the next. New ways of being take time to sink deep roots. Where do I feel called to grow next? What practical steps can I take to become rich soil, ready to produce good fruit thirty or sixty or a hundredfold?

Isaiah 55:10–11
Psalm 65:10,11,12–13,14 (Luke 8:8)
Romans 8:18–23
Matthew 13:1–23 or 13:1–9

Monday

JULY 17

[Jesus said,] "I have come to bring not peace but the sword.
For I have come to set
a man against his father,
a daughter against her mother."
—MATTHEW 10:34–35

Jesus was out to evoke a gut reaction in the apostles—and in us. He's not against loving our parents. He was just being crystal clear on how we must set our priorities. God's will is paramount, and yet we have many complex commitments and all sorts of slippery ways to put a good face on our choices when in reality we're saying, "My will, not Thine, be done." Jesus brought out the sword of discernment to deliver a jolt to help us notice when we put our own agendas first, especially when doing so seems noble, such as caring for parents and family. What's your gut saying?

Exodus 1:8–14,22
Psalm 124:1b–3,4–6,7–8
Matthew 10:34—11:1

Tuesday

JULY 18

• ST. CAMILLUS DE LELLIS, PRIEST •

[Moses] saw an Egyptian striking a Hebrew,
one of his kinsmen.
Looking about and seeing no one,
he slew the Egyptian and hid him in the sand.
—EXODUS 2:11–12

Today's reading from Exodus introduces Moses, the mighty
prophet who would lead the Hebrews out of Egypt to the
Promised Land. I notice in so many biblical accounts that the
steps on the way to achieving God's will lead through mess
and sin. I find that helpful and relieving, because when I look
at my own spiritual path, I see so many stumbles, pitfalls, and
ill-advised detours. But the "through line" of the Bible stories,
and probably yours, is toward a higher way, a way of
forgiveness, fidelity, and love above all. Don't focus only on
your stumblings; revel in how faithfully God keeps lifting
you up and guiding you to a better way.

Exodus 2:1–15a
Psalm 69:3,14,30–31,33–34
Matthew 11:20–24

JULY 19

[Jesus said,] "Although you have hidden these things
from the wise and the learned
you have revealed them to the childlike."
—MATTHEW 11:25

Can you sit with mystery? In my better moments I can. Kids have it easier—everything's a mystery for them, but at some point we begin to feel the need to look savvy and cool. Children are open to wonder and guileless enough to let their inexperience show. They have beginner's mind, which allows them to remain open to the possibility that things may be quite different than they appear. We adults can practice having a childlike attitude, a combination of openness and reliance on a power beyond ourselves. All it takes is willingness to sit with mystery, confident that God will show us wondrous things if we're willing to believe.

Exodus 3:1–6,9–12
Psalm 103:1b–2,3–4,6–7
Matthew 11:25–27

[Moses said,] "When I go to the children of Israel and say to them,
'The God of your fathers has sent me to you,'
if they ask me, 'What is his name?'
what am I to tell them?"
God replied, "I am who am."
—EXODUS 3:13–14

When I first read or heard God's response to Moses, I thought, "Why is he holding back on us with this nonresponsive answer?" But I was missing the point. In essence, God was saying to Moses and to us, "No name can capture who I am. I am a mystery before you. Experience me, and you will come to know who I am." Perhaps we bandy the word *God* around too freely, shrinking it to our level of understanding. To counter that, a friend has lately begun directing his prayers to "Holy Mystery."

Exodus 3:13–20
Psalm 105:1 and 5,8–9,24–25,26–27
Matthew 11:28–30

*His disciples were hungry
and began to pick the heads of grain and eat them.
When the Pharisees saw this, they said to [Jesus],
"See your disciples are doing what is unlawful to
do on the Sabbath."*
—MATTHEW 12:1–2

Consider this story: A seminarian asks his professor, "Is it okay to smoke while praying?" The professor says, "Of course it's not." The next day the seminarian asks, "Is it okay if I pray while having a smoke?" "Of course it is," says the professor. The first instance is about distraction; the other is about intention. Jesus knew the importance of intention, and that caused conflict with the Pharisees. A mature faith can tell if we're seeking a way to drift away from God, or if we are welcoming God into every part of our life.

Exodus 11:10—12:14
Psalm 116:12–13,15 and 16bc,17–18
Matthew 12:1–8

And they said to her, "Woman, why are you weeping?"
She said to them "They have taken my Lord."
—JOHN 20:13

Early in the morning, while it was still dark, Mary Magdalene
strode toward the tomb where they had laid the body of
Jesus. She had stood next to the cross as Jesus died, bearing
his death as faithfully as he had borne his cross. Now it was
quiet, with only the sounds of birds cooing softly. She stood
outside the tomb a long time, weeping—her grief honest and
pure. A man, perhaps a gardener, asked, "Woman, whom are
you looking for?" She urgently explained her mission to find
Jesus. The gardener, who was the risen Jesus, spoke her
name: "Mary!" She rose to the occasion and ran to tell the
others who remained behind, still gathered in fear.

[Feast day reading] Song of Songs 3:1–4b or 2 Corinthians 5:14–17
Psalm 63:2,3-4,5-6,8-9
John 20:1–2,11–18

[Jesus said,] "If you pull up the weeds
you might uproot the wheat along with them."
—MATTHEW 13:29

The first thing to realize is that the wheat and the weeds are
not separate people; they exist in me as an individual. There
are times when I hear the word of God and respond without
hesitation (call me wheat), and there are times when I hear
that same word and resist (uh-oh, now I'm a weed). It can feel
humiliating to be stuck in this cycle of flying high on faith
and unselfconscious loving, then swooping low in selfishness,
anger, resentment, and compulsive behaviors. And yet Jesus
speaks with confidence in the inevitability of the harvest. Do
one thing today to help the wheat grow!

Wisdom 12:13,16–19
Psalm 86:5–6,9–10,15–16 (5a)
Romans 8:26–27
Matthew 13:24–43 or 13:24–30

Monday

JULY 24

• ST. SHARBEL MAKHLŪF, PRIEST •

But Moses answered the people,
"Fear not! Stand your ground,
and you will see the victory the LORD will win
for you today."
—EXODUS 14:13

I should have Moses's words "Stand your ground!" tattooed on my arm. When it comes to trusting in God, I'm a slow learner and a fast forgetter. Like the Hebrews being led to freedom by Moses, my first reaction is to gripe and fear when facing the latest challenge or disruption of my day. I need reminders to unplug the worry machine in my heart and simply trust that things will somehow work out if I but do the next right thing and turn the rest over to the God who had no trouble parting the waters.

Exodus 14:5–18
Exodus 15:1bc–2,3–4,5–6
Matthew 12:38–42

⇒ 240 ⇐

Tuesday

JULY 25

• ST. JAMES, APOSTLE •

*"Command that these two sons of mine sit,
one at your right and the other at your left,
in your Kingdom."*
—MATTHEW 20:21

Once again, people around Jesus got the wrong idea of what
Jesus meant when he spoke of the kingdom of God. The
mother of James and John must have been envisioning a
kingdom like Caesar's, in which commanding was how things
got done. Those wrong ideas continue to this day. Jesus
didn't come to be served but to serve—and even more, to
give up his life for the salvation of the world. It's fine when
parents want wonderful things for their children, but wisdom
teaches that commanding is not a healthy or productive way
to bring it about.

2 Corinthians 4:7–15
Psalm 126:1bc–2ab,2cd–3,4–5,6
Matthew 20:20–28

• ST. JOACHIM AND ST. ANNE, PARENTS OF THE BLESSED VIRGIN MARY •

[Jesus said,] "But some seed fell on rich soil, and produced fruit,
a hundred or sixty or thirtyfold.
Whoever has ears ought to hear."

—MATTHEW 13:9

My four-year-old granddaughter likes to play "Let's pretend."
She's really good at it. Today let's pretend we are rich soil.
Use your imagination. What words come to mind that
describe rich soil? *Receptive, arable, fertile, loamy, prolific,
bountiful, generative, thriving.* What is one thing you could do
today to become richer soil for the word of God? Hint: Jesus
says we have to use our ears.

Exodus 16:1–5,9–15
Psalm 78:18–19,23–24,25–26,27–28
Matthew 13:1–9

JULY 27

*The LORD added, "Go to the people
and have them sanctify themselves
today and tomorrow.
Make them wash their garments and be ready for
the third day."*
—EXODUS 19:10–11

The third day has great significance in the Bible. The first day represents creation, the second is life up until now, the third day represents the end of the old and the beginning of something new. The symbol of the third day echoes from the first chapter of Genesis (on the third day of creation, the dry land appeared, giving forth new life), through the day Moses led the people to meet God at Mount Sinai, to Jesus rising on the third day. In God's time, it is always the third day—the time when new life will emerge and new beginnings can be experienced. Are you ready?

Exodus 19:1–2,9–11,16–20b
Daniel 3:52,53,54,55,56
Matthew 13:10–17

"I, the LORD, am your God,
who brought you out of the Land of Egypt,
that place of slavery.
You shall not have other gods besides me."
—EXODUS 20:2–3

The first commandment reveals something significant about the nature of God—God delivers us from slavery. That's who he is; that's what he does. He frees us to be in relationship with him. He seeks us out where we are exiled and accompanies us to the Promised Land, a place flowing with milk and honey. Whatever is keeping us from giving ourselves to God, whatever stands in the way, he can and will remove. The first commandment reveals God's primary desire—to be in relationship with us. Turn to him when you feel disconnected, lost, and in despair. He'll save you. That's what he does.

Exodus 20:1–17
Psalm 19:8,9,10,11
Matthew 13:18–23

JULY 29

• STS. MARTHA, MARY, AND LAZARUS •

Jesus said to [Martha],
"I am the resurrection and the life;
whoever believes in me, even if he dies, will live,
anyone who lives and believes in me
will never die.
Do you believe this?"
She said to him, "Yes, Lord.
I have come to believe that you are the Christ,
the Son of God."
—JOHN 11:25–27

Martha takes a lot of heat for griping when her sister shirked the housework during Jesus' visit. She deserves better than that. In this golden encapsulation of the essence of the Christian faith, Martha proclaims what she has come to believe. Even as she was cooking and cleaning, she was paying attention and growing in faith. Celebrate her feast today by making dinner for someone you love.

Exodus 24:3–8
Psalm 50:1b–2,5–6,14–15
John 11:19–27 or Luke 10:38–42

Sunday

JULY 30

Jesus said to his disciples,
"The kingdom of heaven is like a treasure buried
in a field,
which a person finds and hides again,
and out of joy goes and sells all that he has
and buys that field."
—MATTHEW 13:44

A friend was celebrating five years' sobriety in Alcoholics Anonymous. I asked, "What's changed during that time?" He said, "New playgrounds, new playmates." Recovery was more than "putting the plug in the jug." It extended to how and where he spent his time (including leaving a job that relied on wining and dining clients) and who he hung around with. Jesus points to the same dynamic when we discover our "buried treasure"—the spiritual core inside us by which we connect with God. We have the initial experience of awakening, we sacrifice what no longer serves, we give all we have so we can live the new life.

1 Kings 3:5,7–12
Psalm 119:57,72,76–77,127–128,129–130 (97a)
Romans 8:28–30
Matthew 13:44–52 or 13:44–46

Monday

JULY 31

• ST. IGNATIUS OF LOYOLA, PRIEST •

They forgot the God who had saved them,
who had done great deeds in Egypt.
—PSALM 106:21

Today is the feast of St. Ignatius of Loyola, whose legacy includes a set of spiritual tools to help us find God in all things and respond wholeheartedly with our lives. One practice he strongly urged was a daily *examen*, which includes these five steps: (1) Get quiet and become aware of God's presence. (2) Review the past twenty-four hours with gratitude. (3) Pay attention to what emotions arise. (4) Choose one feature of the day and pray from it. (5) Look toward tomorrow. You can find more guidance at Ignatianspirituality.com.

Exodus 32:15–24,30–34
Psalm 106:19–20,21–22,23
Matthew 13:31–35

AUGUST 1

The tent, which was called the meeting tent,
Moses used to pitch at some distance away,
outside the camp.
Anyone who wished to consult the LORD
would go to this meeting tent outside the camp.
—EXODUS 33:7

As Moses led the people through the wilderness, he knew
they needed a place set apart to talk with God. Where is
your meeting tent, the place you go to "consult the LORD"? It
doesn't have to be a tent. It may not even be a physical
space. But each of us needs a separate place set aside where
we can connect with God. As a kid, I would climb a mulberry
tree and just be with God. Now I have a spot in my writing
den where I light a candle, get quiet, and enter prayer. And
God is always there, awaiting my arrival.

Exodus 33:7–11; 34:5b–9,28
Psalm 103:6–7,8–9,10–11,12–13
Matthew 13:36–43

Wednesday

AUGUST 2

• ST. EUSEBIUS OF VERCELLI, BISHOP • ST. PETER JULIAN EYMARD, PRIEST •

> *When Aaron, then, and the other children*
> *of Israel saw Moses*
> *and noticed how radiant the skin of his face*
> *had become,*
> *they were afraid to come near him.*
> —EXODUS 34:30

Moses solved the problem of his radiance by wearing a veil after meeting with God. When visiting Sicily years ago, I noticed that people sometimes hung a veil over sacred images. A local waiter told me that these images were too powerful. No one could look at them directly. Laughing, he added, "Maybe we don't want God to see everything we're doing, either!" There seems to be a reluctance built into us that resists letting God come close. Now is a good time to pull back the veil and show God your true face.

Exodus 34:29–35
Psalm 99:5,6,7,9
Matthew 13:44–46

AUGUST 3

> *My soul yearns and pines*
> *for the courts of the LORD.*
> *My heart and my flesh*
> *cry out for the living God.*
> —PSALM 84:3

There is a way that calls you; it's the way of Jesus. There is a truth that beckons; it's the truth of Christ. There is a life that you yearn for; it is the life eternal that flows from the very heart of God. This desiring is itself a divine gift, placed lovingly within us. It is God's GPS, leading us home.

Exodus 40:16–21,34–38
Psalm 84:3,4,5–6a and 8a,11
Matthew 13:47–53

AUGUST 4

• ST. JOHN MARY VIANNEY, PRIEST •

The LORD said to Moses,
"These are the festivals of the LORD
which you shall celebrate
at their proper time with a sacred assembly."
—LEVITICUS 23:1,4

Today's reading comes from the section of Leviticus that establishes laws meant to keep the people holy and ever mindful of the Lord. God himself lays out for Moses the festivals that will form a people and keep God at the center of Jewish life in every season of the year, including the weekly Sabbath, which begins and ends each week around the calendar. Today we celebrate vestiges of these festivals as well as those based on the life, death, resurrection, and ascension of Jesus. We keep them holy so they may keep us holy. Observe, celebrate, remember.

Leviticus 23:1,4–11,15–16,27,34b–37
Psalm 81:3–4,5–6,10–11ab
Matthew 13:54–58

$\mathcal{S}aturday$

AUGUST 5

• THE DEDICATION OF THE BASILICA OF ST. MARY MAJOR •

Herod the tetrarch heard of the reputation of Jesus
and said to his servants, "This man is John
the Baptist.
He has been raised from the dead;
that is why mighty powers are at work in him."
—MATTHEW 14:1–2

Herod was a haunted man. He put John the Baptist in prison for saying that Herod couldn't have his brother's wife, then had John beheaded at the request of his beguiling niece. Not knowing what to do with his guilt, he feared first John, then Jesus. Which makes me grateful that we have the sacrament of reconciliation. Unrepented sin will poison people, causing them to see sin and danger everywhere. That is, everywhere but in themselves. If something's haunting you, it's Saturday, a good time to clean house.

Leviticus 25:1,8–17
Psalm 67:2–3,5,7–8
Matthew 14:1–12

Jesus took Peter, James, and his brother, John,
and led them up a high mountain by themselves.
And he was transfigured before them.
—MATTHEW 17:1–2

Jesus revealed his true identity to the three apostles so they
could accept the hard truths that he must suffer and die. I
relate to Peter's desire to want to set up tents and settle in.
But special mountaintop experiences are not meant to be
souvenirs for our scrapbook or merit badges to flaunt. They
are an opening of our hearts so that we may hear and accept
Jesus's words. We are meant to heed them, which means to
act according to them. The proof of a spiritual experience is
in how we have changed and what we then do afterwards.

Daniel 7:9–10,13–14
Psalm 97:1–2,5–6,9
2 Peter 1:16–19
Matthew 17:1–9

AUGUST 7

*When it was evening, the disciples approached him
and said,
"This is a deserted place and it is already late;
dismiss the crowds so that they can go to the villages
and buy food for themselves."
He said to them, "There is no need for them to go away;
give them some food yourselves."*
—MATTHEW 14:15–16

I can appreciate the disciples' concerns about scarcity of
food. But there's a deeper level of scarcity that Jesus is
addressing. Why do people so often feel as though they have
not enough to offer? I suspect that sort of self-questioning is
why so many people sit quietly when the call for volunteers
goes out. But if we make the simplest effort, we'll often be
amazed at the abundance of energy, effort, and enthusiasm
that arises all around us.

Numbers 11:4b–15
Psalm 81:12–13,14–15,16–17
Matthew 14:13–21

Tuesday

AUGUST 8

• ST. DOMINIC, PRIEST •

Now, Moses himself was by far the meekest man
on the face of the earth.
—NUMBERS 12:3

Say what? Moses, the meekest man in the world? I grew up
watching the formidable Charlton Heston as Moses
challenging Pharoah and staring down the Red Sea, his voice
thundering as he raised his staff to the heavens. Which
makes me realize how important it is to read the words of the
Scriptures firsthand, because so much gets lost (or distorted)
in the translation to movies, books, and even homilies. I see
how Moses was meek, especially in his daily conversations
with God. And I still think of him as the bravest man in the
Hebrew Scriptures, for leading his people from slavery to
freedom.

Numbers 12:1–13
Psalm 51:3–4,5–6ab,6cd–7,12–13
Matthew 14:22–36 or 15:1–2,10–14

⇒ 255 ⇐

AUGUST 9

• ST. TERESA BENEDICTA OF THE CROSS, VIRGIN AND MARTYR •

At this, the whole community broke out with loud cries,
and even in the night the people wailed.
—NUMBERS 14:1

Moses and the people came within sight of the Promised
Land. He sent a scouting group to reconnoiter. They
returned with difficult news: the land was filled with fierce,
unfriendly people. That's when the whole community wailed
into the night. For the past month, the daily readings have
followed the exploits of the Hebrew people, from their
escape from slavery through wandering in the desert. They
faced endless disappointments along the way, and it's not
nearly over yet. What strikes me as this detailed account
unfolds is the need for perseverance, the heart and the will to
struggle on with hope despite setbacks. Hope is the key. Pray
today to keep hope alive and shining in your heart.

Numbers 13:1–2,25—14:1,26–29a,34–35
Psalm 106:6–7ab,13–14,21–22,23
Matthew 15:21–28

AUGUST 10

• ST. LAWRENCE, DEACON AND MARTYR •

Jesus said to his disciples:
"Amen, amen, I say to you,
unless a grain of wheat falls to the ground and dies,
it remains just a grain of wheat;
but if it dies, it produces much fruit."
—JOHN 12:24

When Jesus begins a message with "Amen, amen I say to you," he signals that what comes next is important and it comes straight from the Father. Today's Gospel on this feast of St. Lawrence, martyr, conveys a central tenet of Christian life. We must die—to self, to our ego, and to our sins if we hope to rise to a new way of living grounded in God. This paradox—dying so we may live—is hard to comprehend. Rather than think our way into living this principle, we need to live our way into new thinking, by dying to ourselves one small death at a time.

2 Corinthians 9:6–10
Psalm 112:1–2,5–6,7–8,9
John 12:24–26

Friday

AUGUST 11

• ST. CLARE, VIRGIN •

I remember the deeds of the LORD;
yes, I remember your wonders of old.
And I meditate on your works;
your exploits I ponder.
—PSALM 77:12–13

Today's psalm encourages us to remember the many blessings we've received from the heart of God. Make a timeline of the past six months, and jot down a few of the times you felt the presence of God, or times you recognized God's providence in your life. Spend time remembering, and let your remembering turn into pondering so you can more deeply understand and appreciate the goodness of the Lord.

Deuteronomy 4:32–40
Psalm 77:12–13,14–15,16 and 21
Matthew 16:24–28

Saturday

AUGUST 12

• ST. JANE FRANCES DE CHANTAL, RELIGIOUS •

Hear, O Israel! The LORD is our God,
the LORD alone!
Therefore, you shall love the LORD, your God,
with all your heart,
and with all your soul,
and with all your strength.
—DEUTERONOMY 6:4–5

These words are the essence of the Hebrew Scriptures, asserting that there is one God, not many, and our response is to love the Lord completely, with our entire being. Because there is only one God, there is only one intelligence behind creation and one purpose for our lives. Jewish parents teach their children to say this prayer as they go to sleep at night. Pray it now aloud. Certainly, Jesus and the apostles grew up saying this prayer. It's in our DNA.

Deuteronomy 6:4–13
Psalm 18:2–3a,3c–4,47 and 51
Matthew 17:14–20

⋺ 259 ⋹

AUGUST 13

• NINETEENTH SUNDAY IN ORDINARY TIME •

At the mountain of God, Horeb,
Elijah came to a cave where he took shelter.
—1 KINGS 19:9,11

Elijah was seeking escape. He felt like a failure as a prophet and was in fear for his life. Wanting to hide, he found just the cave in which to escape the dangers closing in on him. God beckoned Elijah out of the cave, saying that he would be passing by. There came a wind so strong it crushed rocks, but the Lord was not in the wind. Nor was the Lord in the earthquake or the fire that appeared next. God was in a tiny sound, a whisper uttered heart to heart. When we're in desolation, it's hard to quiet our mind and heart enough to hear what God is whispering to us. Sometimes we just need to find a handy cave.

1 Kings 19:9a,11–13a
Psalm 85:9,10,11–12,13–14
Romans 9:1–5
Matthew 14:22–33

Moses said to the people:
"And now, Israel, what does the LORD, your God,
ask of you
but to fear the LORD, your God, and follow
his ways exactly,
to love and serve the LORD, your God,
with all your heart and all your soul,
to keep the commandments and statutes of the LORD
which I enjoin on you today for your own good?"
—DEUTERONOMY 10:12–13

For our own good? When we can recognize that God's commandments are, in fact, not just for our own good but also for our own joy, wellness, and satisfaction, we will have reached a stage of spiritual maturity. Lord, help me grow in wisdom so that I may eagerly follow your ways.

Deuteronomy 10:12–22
Psalm 147:12–13,14–15,19–20
Matthew 17:22–27

Tuesday

AUGUST 15

• THE ASSUMPTION OF THE BLESSED VIRGIN MARY •

A woman from the crowd called out and said to [Jesus],
"Blessed is the womb that carried you
and the breasts at which you nursed."
He replied,
"Rather, blessed are those
who hear the word of God and observe it."
—LUKE 11:27–28

Mary, whose assumption into heaven we celebrate today,
qualifies on both counts. She was the mother who carried
Jesus in her womb, and she heard the word of God and
observed it, even before Jesus was conceived. Her yes
qualifies her as the first disciple. What yes can I make today,
Lord, that will help your will be done?

VIGIL:
1 Chronicles 15:3–4,15–16; 16:1–2
Psalm 132:6–7,9–10,13–14
1 Corinthians 15:54b–57
Luke 11:27–28

DAY:
Revelation 11:19a; 12:1–6a,10ab
Psalm 45:10,11,12,16
1 Corinthians 15:20–27
Luke 1:39–56

Wednesday

AUGUST 16

• ST. STEPHEN OF HUNGARY •

Jesus said to his disciples:
"If your brother sins against you,
go and tell him his fault between you and him alone."
—MATTHEW 18:15

I looked very closely, but Jesus never advised, "If your brother sins against you, tell everyone about it but him." Nor did it say, "A great way to spend a lunch hour at work is talking about someone who's not present." It's so easy to talk about our problems with other people—with everybody *but* the person we're having the trouble with. Gossip is corrosive. Sometimes at home, work, or at church we confuse surface niceness with honest love. Be courageous, talk openly to those you feel have wronged you; then, just as openly, listen to their reply.

Deuteronomy 34:1–12
Psalm 66:1–3a,5 and 8,16–17
Matthew 18:15–20

AUGUST 17

The LORD said to Joshua,
"Today I will begin to exalt you in the sight
of all Israel,
that they may know I am with you,
as I was with Moses."
—JOSHUA 3:7

The Lord spoke these words to Joshua as he prepared to accompany the people into the Promised Land. They walked in on solid ground because the Lord parted the waters of the Jordan, as he had done with the Red Sea. This time, Moses was not with them. He was given the gift of seeing the holy destination he aimed for, for forty years. But he never set foot upon that land. It was the Ark of the Covenant, the presence of Yahweh, that led the way. We all can play a part in God's great story of salvation, but God is the author and the protagonist.

Joshua 3:7–10a,11,13–17
Psalm 114:1–2,3–4,5–6
Matthew 18:21–19:1

AUGUST 18

Give thanks to the LORD OF LORDS,
for his mercy endures forever. . . .
Who led his people through the wilderness,
for his mercy endures forever.
—PSALM 136:3,16

The story of Exodus, in which God rescued the Israelites from bondage, fed them in the desert, gave them rules to live according to his will, and led them to the Promised Land, is an archetype. That means that the basic elements of that story echo throughout history even to the level of individual lives. So much is in flux today that it's easy to fear we are lost in the wilderness, uncertain of God's presence in events around us, global or extremely local. The Hebrews freely raised their complaints to God. We, too, should raise our concerns because God is merciful. And his mercy endures forever.

Joshua 24:1–13
Psalm 136:1–3,16–18,21–22 and 24
Matthew 19:3–12

Saturday

AUGUST 19

• ST. JOHN EUDES, PRIEST •

Children were brought to Jesus
that he might lay his hands on them and pray.
The disciples rebuked them, but Jesus said,
"Let the children come to me, and do not
prevent them;
for the Kingdom of heaven belongs to such as these."
—MATTHEW 19:13–14

What can we learn about faith from children? We can learn to say we're afraid when life gets scary. We can learn to say we're sorry when we've done wrong. And do what we can to comfort others when they're hurting or sad. We can learn to trust that when we call out, someone will be there. And we can learn that we can never do all this perfectly but we can always try and try again.

Joshua 24:14–29
Psalm 16:1–2a and 5,7–8,11
Matthew 19:13–15

———————

The woman came and did Jesus homage, saying,
"Lord, help me."
He said in reply,
"It is not right to take the food of the children
and throw it to the dogs."
She said, "Please, Lord for even the dogs eat the scraps
that fall from the table of their masters."
Then Jesus said to her in reply,
"O woman, great is your faith!"
—MATTHEW 15:25–28

The Canaanite woman's mission—to heal her daughter—arose
from love. Jesus' mission also flowed from love. They were
separated by gender, nationality, and religious tradition. The
woman disregarded those differences because she recognized a
greater similarity they shared. Her faith was revealed in her
courage, perseverance, and creativity. Focus first on your
similarities with others instead of on the differences.

Isaiah 56:1,6–7
Psalm 67:2–3,5,6,8 (4)
Romans 11:13–15,29–32
Matthew 15:21–28

AUGUST 21

• ST. PIUS X, POPE •

When the young man heard this statement,
he went away sad,
for he had many possessions.
—MATTHEW 19:22

I've always felt sad for this young man, mainly because I can identify with him so well. It's natural for young people to try to impress, to shine a light on their good and honorable accomplishments, and stuff the faults, foibles, and self-doubts into their shadow. So when Jesus's answer, offered out of love, addressed the young man's real spiritual challenge—pride of possessions—he went away sad. My prayer for him (and it's also a prayer for myself) is that he returned to Jesus often. And I believe it was Jesus's prayer as well.

Judges 2:11–19
Psalm 106:34–35,36–37,39–40,43ab and 44
Matthew 19:16–22

AUGUST 22

• THE QUEENSHIP OF THE BLESSED VIRGIN MARY •

[Jesus said,] "Again I say to you,
it is easier for a camel to pass through the eye
of a needle
than for one who is rich to enter
the Kingdom of God."
—MATTHEW 19:24

There's a saying that if you ask people what level of wealth
constitutes being rich, they will always respond, "Twenty
percent more than I have." Another saying goes, "You can
never acquire enough of that which won't satisfy you." Thus,
we have a vicious circle. Jesus' image is very effective: a
camel, a large and unruly beast normally bundled with
burdens, versus a needle's eye. No way! The key is to let go
of our attachment to the burdens so that we are no longer
camels and the gate of heaven no longer appears as tiny as
the eye of a needle.

Judges 6:11–24a
Psalm 85:9,11–12,13–14
Matthew 19:23–30

"Summon the laborers and give them their pay,
beginning with the last and ending with the first."
When those who had started about five o'clock came,
each received the usual daily wage.
So when the first came, they thought
that they would receive more,
but each of them also got the usual wage.
And on receiving it they grumbled against
the landowner.
—MATTHEW 20:8-11

So how do you feel about the outcome of this parable where those who worked a full day received the same pay as those who worked less than half that time? Does it offend your sense of fairness? God measures using a different scale than we often do. One lesson I take from this parable is "Don't count what you didn't get, be grateful for what you do get and all that you've already gotten: your life, his grace, and the promise of eternal life."

Judges 9:6–15
Psalm 21:2–3,4–5,6–7
Matthew 20:1–16

Thursday

AUGUST 24

· • ST. BARTHOLOMEW, APOSTLE • ·

*But Nathanael said to him,
"Can anything good come from Nazareth?"
Philip said to him, "Come and see."'*
—JOHN 1:46

One of the best things in dealing with people is that they
will often surprise you—for the better. We may negatively
judge others (if only subconsciously) by the way they dress,
their style of speech, family of origin, or other externals, only
to have the reality of what they do or say shatter our
negative expectations. The person I expect to be antagonistic
shows up to be warm and congenial, the one I feared would
be shallow shows a rare depth, and the one I assume is
self-centered and demanding is extremely kind, helpful, and
self-deprecating. Like Jesus, we are more than meets the eye.
"Come and see."

Revelation 21:9b–14
Psalm 145:10–11,12–13,17–18
John 1:45–51

≥ 271 ≤

The LORD keeps faith forever,
secures justice for the oppressed,
gives food to the hungry.
The LORD sets captives free.
—PSALM 146:6–7

If you want to know what's on God's mind, read the Psalms. It's impressive how often the Psalms and other Old Testament Scriptures focus on God's passion for justice. God sees that those who are oppressed are treated justly, that the hungry do not go away empty, and that those exiled in captivity see freedom. These themes show up regularly. So when you say, "Thy will be done," know that these are the issues God continuously has in mind.

Ruth 1:1,3–6,14b–16,22
Psalm 146:5–6ab,6c–7,8–9a,9bc–10
Matthew 22:34–40

Ruth the Moabite said to Naomi,
"Let me go and glean ears of grain in the field
of anyone who will allow me that favor."
Naomi said to her, "Go, my daughter."
—RUTH 2:2

Ruth was a faithful and loving daughter-in-law who stood by Naomi, her widowed mother-in-law, left her family, and accompanied Naomi to an unknown land. She was also a Moabite who, because of her generosity and fidelity, became the great-grandmother of King David. Lineage and nationality can divide people and turn them against one another. In Ruth's case, devoted love overcame the divisions and became yet another instance of God writing straight with crooked lines. Be ready today to find God's surprises where you least expect them.

Ruth 2:1–3,8–11; 4:13–17
Psalm 128:1b–2,3,4,5
Matthew 23:1–12

AUGUST 27

• TWENTY-FIRST SUNDAY IN ORDINARY TIME •

*Oh, the depth of riches and wisdom and
knowledge of God!
How inscrutable are his judgments and
how unsearchable his ways!*
—ROMANS 11:33

St. Paul's acclamation of God's vast and unknowable wisdom
cuts both ways. It can be amazingly comforting or terribly
frustrating and even angering, depending on how much we
are able to trust in God. Some people can't get past the
not-knowing. But direct experience of God's love makes it
possible to trust that whatever is unfolding is moved by love,
intention, and benign purpose. An old adage says, "We can
see the seeds in an apple, but only God sees the apples
contained in the seeds." Faith, love, and acceptance give a
foretaste of the apples that have not yet blossomed.

Isaiah 22:19–23
Psalm 138:1–2,2–3,6,8 (8bc)
Romans 11:33–36
Matthew 16:13–20

AUGUST 28

Paul, Silvanus, and Timothy to the church of
the Thessalonians
in God the Father and the Lord Jesus Christ:
grace to you and peace.
—1 THESSALONIANS 1:1

In his epistles to the far-flung Christian communities he had established, St. Paul would often have to deal with thorny issues. And he wasn't one to shy away from conflict. Yet he typically began his messages to the fledgling Christians by wishing them peace and reminding them from where that peace would flow—God's own self. Think about that the next time you face a difficult meeting at work, at home, or in your neighborhood. Begin by finding God's peace in yourself and wishing that peace on all who will be involved. Set your inner disposition solidly on God, and you invite the Holy Spirit to flow freely in your midst.

1 Thessalonians 1:1–5,8b–10
Psalm 149:1b–2,3–4,5–6a and 9b
Matthew 23:13–22

AUGUST 29

• THE PASSION OF ST. JOHN THE BAPTIST •

With such affection for you, we were determined
to share with you
not only the Gospel of God,
but our very selves as well,
so dearly beloved had you become to us.
—1 THESSALONIANS 2:8

Years ago I read a story about an outreach program to help people at risk of losing their homes. Of the groups funded to execute the plan, one group outperformed all others. The program sponsors investigated and discovered that the leading group was a community of Catholic nuns, and the deciding difference in their performance was personal care. The sisters lived among the people, knew their names, stories, and circumstances, and cared about each one individually. Who do you live among? Where can your care make a difference for good?

1 Thessalonians 2:1–8
Psalm 139:1–3,4–6
Mark 6:17–29

AUGUST 30

If I take the wings of the dawn,
if I settle at the farthest limits of the sea,
Even there your hand shall guide me,
and your right hand hold me fast.
—PSALM 139:9–10

Sometimes you'll hear a desolate place described as a "godforsaken land." But there is no such thing, just as there are no godforsaken people. Our circumstances can be difficult, but we are never distant from the loving care of God. A few times in my life I have felt beyond the reach of goodness, abandoned by God. Difficult circumstances I faced seemed insurmountable. From the distance of time, I now recognize that when I most feared I had left God behind, God's hand was still guiding me. His grace was present, and divine providence was leading me home.

1 Thessalonians 2:9–13
Psalm 139:7–8,9–10,11–12ab
Matthew 23:27–32

AUGUST 31

*What thanksgiving, then, can we render to God for you,
for all the joy we feel on your account before our God?*
—1 THESSALONIANS 3:9

Whether you get your news online, via television or radio, or,
like me, in print-like dinosaurs such as newspapers and
magazines, most days the stories present a steady stream of
corrupt politicians, nefarious criminals, greedy business
leaders, and general ne'er-do-wells. You can get to wondering
if everyone's a crook. Remedy that by making a list of people
you know who are genuinely good. Granted, none of us is
perfect, but some people walk through life leaving things
better than when they arrived. Make your list. Feel the
goodness. Know that there are countless others around the
world who fit that category. Thank God for their presence in
the world.

1 Thessalonians 3:7–13
Psalm 90:3–5a,12–13,14 and 17
Matthew 24:42–51

Therefore, stay awake,
for you know neither the day nor the hour.
—MATTHEW 25:13

Late one December evening, I was walking through downtown Chicago, head down, lost in my own concerns. A bus stopped in front of me, and off came a grandmother and her six- or seven-year-old grandson. The boy stopped, looked all around at the abundant Christmas lights and decorations, and said, quite dramatically, "Whoa! Who did all that?" And for the first time that season I looked up and took in the sights that had lit him up in awe. I had been sleepwalking, but thanks to this little Christmas herald, I came to my senses just in time.

1 Thessalonians 4:1–8
Psalm 97:1 and 2b,5–6,10,11–12
Matthew 25:1–13

Saturday

SEPTEMBER 2

[The servant said,] "Master, I knew you were a demanding person,
harvesting where you did not plant
and gathering where you did not scatter;
so out of fear I went off and buried your talent
in the ground."
—MATTHEW 25:24–25

The writers of the Gospels understood the great power of
fear, considering it to be the major underlying obstacle to
spiritual growth. Pay attention to your own life, and witness
how prevalent fear is and how often it masquerades as greed
(fear of not having enough), embarrassment (fear of not
being enough), anger (a response to my own fears being
revealed), grief (fear of great loss), or many other instances
of looking for security, sufficiency, and love in all the wrong
places. The cure to fear is faith, an active embracing of God's
gifts and turning them into goodness for all.

1 Thessalonians 4:9–11
Psalm 98:1,7–8,9
Matthew 25:14–30

Sunday

SEPTEMBER 3

• TWENTY-SECOND SUNDAY IN ORDINARY TIME •

Then Jesus said to his disciples,
"Whoever wishes to come after me must deny himself,
take up his cross, and follow me.
For whoever wishes to save his life will lose it."
—MATTHEW 16:24–25

What makes it possible to "take up our cross"? First, we must be free to make that choice, which means to deny ourselves. We're not denying the self that is created in God's image and likeness. We're denying the ego that attaches to an array of substitutes for grace, thus attempting to be our own savior. By saying no to those strategies of attachment, we lose our "old life" and can take up our cross. Ask yourself, "What does today's cross look like, and what stands in my way of taking it up?"

Jeremiah 20:7–9
Psalm 63:2,3–4,5–6,8–9 (2b)
Romans 12:1–2
Matthew 16:21–27

⋟ 281 ⋞

[Jesus] unrolled the scroll and found the passage
where it was written:
The Spirit of the Lord is upon me,
because he has anointed me
to bring glad tidings to the poor.
—LUKE 4:17–18

Jesus returned to his hometown, entered the synagogue, and quite purposely read this passage from the book of Isaiah. He was making a point, revealing that he is the one Isaiah was referring to. He had already been proclaiming liberty to captives and restoring sight to the blind. But his neighbors had already decided he was merely the son of Joseph, the carpenter, and where did he get off talking this way about himself? Who have I pegged as someone of no consequence? Who, today, am I underestimating?

1 Thessalonians 4:13–18
Psalm 96:1 and 3,4–5,11–12,13
Luke 4:16–30

SEPTEMBER 5

*In the synagogue there was a man with the spirit
of an unclean demon,
and he cried out in a loud voice,
"What have you to do with us, Jesus of Nazareth?
Have you come to destroy us?
I know who you are—the Holy One of God!"*
—LUKE 4:33–34

Jesus left his hometown, where people couldn't see beyond
his humble beginnings, and went to Capernaum, where
everyone was astonished by him, including a demon who
recognized him as "the Holy One of God." When our sinful
or selfish attachments are challenged, our own inner demons
are often the first to speak out in protest. But if we faithfully
practice the presence of God, a quieter voice inside affords us
the strength to say "Yes, Lord, thy will, not mine, be done."

1 Thessalonians 5:1–6,9–11
Psalm 27:1,4,13–14
Luke 4:31–37

Wednesday

SEPTEMBER 6

*I, like a green olive tree
in the house of God,
Trust in the mercy of God
forever and ever.*
—PSALM 52:10–11

Rooted. That's how we are to be: rooted in God, gathering up
strength to produce good fruit. In the Mediterranean world,
olive trees are an essential source of life, healing, and hope.
They are living symbols of God's loving care, always and
everywhere close at hand. They live a long time, producing
fruit year after year. Where are you rooted? Who or what feeds
your soul, influencing the fruit your life produces?

Colossians 1:1–8
Psalm 52:10,11
Luke 4:38–44

SEPTEMBER 7

After [Jesus] had finished speaking, he said to Simon,
"Put out into deep water and lower your nets
for a catch."
—LUKE 5:4

Jesus wanted Simon and his crew to go out far on the lake
and lower their nets deeper than they had been used to. He
was giving them an indication of what their new role as
fishers of men would entail. So often we live on the surface
of life. But Jesus came to address the woundedness we all
have in our depths, the hurts and failures that make us
vulnerable to sin to the point where we cling to it rather than
gladly receive redemption. The healing Jesus offers goes
deep. Are we willing to meet him there?

Colossians 1:9–14
Psalm 98:2–3ab,3cd–4,5–6
Luke 5:1–11

Friday

SEPTEMBER 8

Behold, the virgin shall be with child and bear a son,
and they shall name him Emmanuel,
which means "God is with us."
—MATTHEW 1:23

In the Scriptures, the word *behold* is a call to pay deeper attention, a warning that what follows in the sentence is a manifestation of God. It's the nudge in the ribs, the side glance that says, "You won't want to miss this!" Today's use of *behold* lets us know that this is no usual birth announcement. Something big happened here, so slow it down, open your eyes and mind, and, wordlessly, take it in and let it speak to your heart. Some events shouldn't be reduced to a passing glance. The coming of our Savior in our midst is surely one of them. Behold!

Micah 5:1–4a or Romans 8:28–30
Psalm 13:6ab,6c
Matthew 1:1–16,18–23 or 1:18–23

SEPTEMBER 9

• ST. PETER CLAVER, PRIEST •

Behold, God is my helper;
the Lord sustains my life.
Freely will I offer you sacrifice;
I will praise your name, O LORD, for its goodness.
—PSALM 54:6 AND 8

Praise can cut both ways. We know instantly when someone
is too effusive with phony praise. And we can recognize
when someone is genuine in their compliments. Praise must
flow from honest appreciation of the other. And in God's
case, piling on a thesaurus-full of superlatives is not what's
called for. We must spend the time opening our hearts and
minds to all that God has wrought—creation itself, the
people we love, our own potential for love and goodness—so
that praise may rise up naturally, carrying us ever closer to
God's own heart.

Colossians 1:21–23
Psalm 54:3–4,6 and 8
Luke 6:1–5

SEPTEMBER 10

• TWENTY-THIRD SUNDAY IN ORDINARY TIME •

*[Jesus said,] "If your brother sins against you,
go and tell him his fault between you and him alone.
If he listens to you, you have won over your brother."*
—MATTHEW 18:15

In his teaching and in his actions, Jesus often expressed a relentless desire for reconciliation. Consider his parable of the lost sheep, or today's Gospel reading on restoring peace within the church. Reconciliation requires certain skills that aren't necessarily found widely in our communities—or in ourselves. Reconciliation requires (1) self-awareness and the ability to articulate in a noninflammatory way why I am feeling offended; (2) honest and humble recognition of what my part is in this situation; and (3) a stronger desire for reconciliation than for being proven right. These don't come easily, yet acquiring them is a spiritual practice that can heal the world.

Ezekiel 33:7–9
Psalm 95:1–2,6–7,8–9 (8)
Romans 13:8–10
Matthew 18:15–20

SEPTEMBER 11

Only in God be at rest, my soul,
for from him comes my hope.
He alone is my rock and my salvation,
my stronghold; I shall not be disturbed.
—PSALM 62:6–7

Rest. Some days it feels as if there is no rest to be found. The demands of life press on us; our inner worries abound. Where can we find the rest we so long for? St. Augustine provides this insight: "You have made us for yourself, O Lord, and our hearts are restless until they rest in you." So often what makes us restless is a deficiency of hope. Yet if we accept our true identities as beloved daughters and sons of God, we'll be at rest because our hope is secured. We are made for God, and God will never abandon us.

Colossians 1:24—2:3
Psalm 62:6–7,9
Luke 6:6–11

Everyone in the crowd sought to touch him
because power came forth from him
and healed them all.
—LUKE 6:19

Healing. What within you needs healing? Imagine yourself in
today's Gospel, where Jesus comes down the mountain after a
night in prayer and communion with the Father. He walks
out onto the plain and is surrounded by a great crowd of
people, all acknowledging their pain and their physical and
spiritual ailments. "Even those tormented with unclean spirits
were cured," says Luke (6:18). Imagine you are there.
Approach Jesus and ask for the healing you need. Imagine
that Jesus sees you and hears you. He touches you, and
power comes forth from him. Open your heart to it. Thank
him for coming near.

Colossians 2:6–15
Psalm 145:1b–2,8–9,10–11
Luke 6:12–19

But woe to you who are rich,
for you have received your consolation.
—LUKE 6:24

The Beatitudes talk about what leads to blessedness. But they also speak about what leads to woe—giving examples of those who are rich, sated, happy, and being spoken well of. Such people risk the sin of self-sufficiency. The antidote to "the woes" is to take an honest account of your blessings.

Begin with the life you were born into: the family, the society, the times. Think of those who educated you and the great logistical infrastructure that makes it certain you can open your refrigerator and always have a delectable array of choices before you. The list is endless. Thank the One who created you and the world you live in. It's all gift.

Colossians 3:1–11
Psalm 145:2–3,10–11,12–13ab
Luke 6:20–26

For God did not send his Son into the world
to condemn the world,
but that the world might be saved through him.
—JOHN 3:17

Jesus didn't come to earth to condemn us. He came to give us a way out. He said, in essence, "Whatever condition has you stuck, it doesn't have to be like this. There is a way out. A way out of your selfishness, a way out of your compulsive behaviors, a way out of your fear, your anger, your despair." God wants you to be happy, holy, joyous, and free. He sent his Son to show us the way.

Numbers 21:4b–9
Psalm 78:1bc–2,34–35,36–37,38
Philippians 2:6–11
John 3:13–17

*[Simeon said to Mary,] "This child is destined
for the fall and rise of many in Israel,
and to be a sign that will be contradicted
and you yourself a sword will pierce
so that the thoughts of many hearts may be revealed."*
—LUKE 2:34–35

During World War II, with so many young people stationed overseas in harm's way, the Novena to the Sorrowful Mother attracted so many people in Chicago, especially mothers of soldiers, that churches used mounted police to handle crowd control. As an altar boy in the 1960s, I was frequently assigned to serve at that same Novena in our parish and came to see the truth in Simeon's prediction that Mary's sorrow would help reveal the thoughts (and concerns) of many hearts. What do you do with your sorrow? To whom do you turn?

1 Timothy 1:1–2, 12–14
Psalm 16:1b–2a and 5, 7–8, 11
John 19:25–27 or Luke 2:33–35

[Jesus said,] "I will show you what someone is like who comes to me,
listens to my words, and acts on them.
That one is like a man building a house,
who dug deeply and laid the foundation on rock."
—LUKE 6:47–48

St. Luke is keen on people not just listening to Jesus' words but also taking them to heart and acting on them. Action flowing from faith is the foundation that helps us withstand temptations and remain unwavering in the face of life's challenges. Experience has taught me that the action I most need to take daily is to begin my day with prayer. Prayer opens my mind and heart and will to all the ways God is working on my behalf throughout the day. And that's a firm foundation.

1 Timothy 1:15–17
Psalm 113:1b–2,3–4,5a and 6–7
Luke 6:43–49

SEPTEMBER 17

• TWENTY-FOURTH SUNDAY IN ORDINARY TIME •

Peter approached Jesus and asked him,
"Lord, if my brother sins against me,
how often must I forgive?
As many as seven times?"
—MATTHEW 18:21–22

God's default position toward us is mercy, which opens up for us a life unencumbered by the effects of sin. Having received God's mercy, how then shall we respond? Jesus warns us to extend mercy outward for the good of the world and the saving of our souls. Refusing to extend mercy toward others makes it dry up for us as well. We are meant to live in a world of reconciliation. So, when Peter asked what he must have thought was a very magnanimous question, what Jesus heard him asking was, "When can I get back to the delicious world of vengeance?" To which Jesus responded, "Not on my watch."

Sirach 27:30—28:7
Psalm 103:1–2,3–4,9–10,11–12 (8)
Romans 14:7–9
Matthew 18:21–35

Monday

SEPTEMBER 18

And Jesus went with them,
but when he was only a short distance from the house,
the centurion sent friends to tell him,
"Lord, do not trouble yourself,
for I am not worthy to have you enter under my roof.
Therefore, I did not consider myself worthy
to come to you;
but say the word and let my servant be healed."
—LUKE 7:6–7

We pray a version of the centurion's words at Mass. In Jesus' time, to enter under someone's roof was to enter their whole world. Everything within was made available to the visitor. And I think that's where the real challenge lies each week when we gather in prayer. Am I willing to invite Jesus into all parts of my life? Or am I keeping some parts of myself separate and unreachable? Pray for the grace to open your whole life and self to his loving care.

1 Timothy 2:1–8
Psalm 28:2,7,8–9
Luke 7:1–10

I will persevere in the way of integrity;
when will you come to me?
—PSALM 101:2

In two short phrases, the psalmist promises to persevere in the way of integrity, a necessary virtue in the life of a Christian, and affirms his faith that God will come to his aid. In this short verse, we see the dynamic of how faith works: we can persevere in doing our part because we know God always does his. In fact, it is God's initiative that planted such faith and awareness in our hearts. Today, look for ways you can persevere in integrity, even when tempted to do otherwise. Thank God for the desire to persevere and for the grace to carry it out.

1 Timothy 3:1–13
Psalm 101:1b–2ab,2cd–3ab,5,6
Luke 7:11–17

Wednesday

SEPTEMBER 20

• ST. ANDREW KIM TAE-GŎN, PRIEST, AND ST. PAUL CHŎNG HA-SANG, AND
COMPANIONS, MARTYRS •

*[Jesus said,] "For John the Baptist came neither eating food
nor drinking wine,
and you said, 'He is possessed by a demon.'
The Son of Man came eating and drinking
and you said,
'Look, he is a glutton and a drunkard,
a friend of tax collectors and sinners.'"*
—LUKE 7:33–34

Jesus and John the Baptist were both targets of criticism
based on totally opposite complaints. And in each case, the
criticisms missed the point of what each of them was trying
to do—encourage true repentance on the one hand and
announce the Good News of salvation on the other. You may
experience unfair criticism when trying to do something
good in the world. Just know you're not the first and, in fact,
you're in good company.

1 Timothy 3:14–16
Psalm 111:1–2,3–4,5–6
Luke 7:31–35

SEPTEMBER 21

[Jesus] heard this and said,
"Those who are well do not need a physician,
but the sick do.
Go and learn the meaning of the words,
I desire mercy, not sacrifice.
—MATTHEW 9:12–13

Jesus walked into a town where there were two large buildings. Outside one it said, "Sinners Here," and outside the other it said, "Already Saved." Which one do you think Jesus would enter? As it turns out, he entered both but was criticized for consorting with sinners. Is it any wonder he pursued the lost? Is there any reason our parishes (and we) shouldn't do the same?

Ephesians 4:1–7,11–13
Psalm 19:2–3,4–5
Matthew 9:9–13

SEPTEMBER 22

*Those who want to be rich are falling
into temptation and into a trap
and into many foolish and harmful desires,
which plunge them into ruin and destruction.
For the love of money is the root of all evils.*
—1 TIMOTHY 6:9–10

In his letters to the church communities he founded, St. Paul ends up addressing many issues and temptations the fledgling groups face. Today he deals with the desire to accumulate riches that is driving some members into temptation. In today's Gospel reading we hear of "some women" who accompanied Jesus and provided for him and the apostles "out of their resources." Do I love money as an end in itself, or do I use money to facilitate new life and goodness?

1 Timothy 6:2c–12
Psalm 49:6–7,8–10,17–18,19–20
Luke 8:1–3

• ST. PIUS OF PIETRELCINA, PRIEST •

[Jesus said,] "But as for the seed that fell on rich soil,
they are the ones who, when they have heard
the word,
embrace it with a generous and good heart,
and bear fruit through perseverance."
—LUKE 8:15

A famous violinist was walking through Manhattan when a
tourist asked, "How do you get to Carnegie Hall?" The
musician responded, "Practice, practice, practice." What does
it take to make significant change in our lives instead of
making grand resolutions that quickly evaporate? Practices. To
lose a bad habit, create a new one in its place. To stop
gossiping, come prepared with "good news" stories you can
tell. To end a habit of resentment toward a person, pray for
that person every time the resentment arises. Ask for God's
grace and get creative as you consistently swap virtue for vice.

1 Timothy 6:13–16
Psalm 100:1b–2,3,4,5
Luke 8:4–15

The LORD is near to all who call upon him,
to all who call upon him in truth.
—PSALM 145:18

A professor in my Ignatian Spirituality class told us about a man who prayed, asking God to take away his resentment at a relative, without success. The professor said, "Show me how you pray." The man, looking very fervent, lifted his head to the heavens and repeated over and over, "God, take this resentment away from me!" The professor looked at the man's hands, which were clenched tight. He said, "Your words are saying you want to let this go, but your hands are telling a different story." The man opened his hands and prayed again, and relief came to his face. Sometimes our body knows more than our mind is willing to acknowledge.

Isaiah 55:6–9
Psalm 145:2–3,8–9,17–18 (18a)
Philippians 1:20c–24,27a
Matthew 20:1–16a

Jesus said to the crowd:
"No one who lights a lamp conceals it with a vessel
or sets it under a bed;
rather, he places it on a lampstand
so that those who enter may see the light."
—LUKE 8:16

The nice thing about light is that you don't have to force it on anyone; you just have to let it shine. How do we let the light of Christ shine in us? By living in the light, which means turning away from those things that keep us in darkness (selfishness, dishonesty, and fear, for example), and taking actions of faith, hope, and love toward others. Call to mind three people in your life who have been a beacon of light to you. Say a prayer of gratitude for them, and let your light shine.

Ezra 1:1–6
Psalm 126:1b–2ab,2cd–3,4–5,6
Luke 8:16–18

SEPTEMBER 26

• ST. COSMAS AND ST. DAMIAN, MARTYRS •

The Levites, every one of whom had purified himself
for the occasion,
sacrificed the Passover for the rest of the exiles.
—EZRA 6:20

Today is the feast of Sts. Cosmas and Damian, twin brothers born in Arabia in the third century who were physicians who spread faith in Jesus and healed people for free. Little is known about them except through legends, and yet they are mentioned in the first eucharistic prayer at Mass, and Catholics around the world remain devoted to them. From the time of their martyrdom people have turned to them for help and urged others to do so. People who live and die according to their convictions and because of their faith give hope to the world long after their deaths.

Ezra 6:7–8,12b,14–20
Psalm 122:1–2,3–4ab,4cd–5
Luke 8:19–21

> [Jesus] said to them, "Take nothing for the journey,
> neither walking stick, nor sack, nor food, nor money,
> and let no one take a second tunic."
> —LUKE 9:3

When I got my first job in Catholic publishing, I immediately
went out and bought a full-length leather coat, a color and
style that were popular for about a week and a half in the late
seventies. I clearly did not trust that my faith in God was
sufficient "cover" for my fear of stepping into this great new
opportunity. Before shopping, I should have taken to heart
Jesus' instructions to the apostles in today's Gospel. But I heard
Jesus' warning to rely only on God every time I saw that unused
coat smirking at me from the front hall closet.

Ezra 9:5–9
Tobit 13:2,3–4a,4befghn,7–8
Luke 9:1–6

Thursday

SEPTEMBER 28

Thus says the Lord of hosts:
Consider your ways!
You have sown much, but have brought in little;
you have eaten, but have not been satisfied;
You have drunk, but have not been exhilarated;
have clothed yourselves, but not
been warmed;
And whoever earned wages
earned them for a bag with holes in it.
—HAGGAI 1:5–6

Spend time today contemplating the prophet Haggai's description of life when we don't align our actions to God's will. God desires more for us, and we will find it if we first just seek his ways.

Haggai 1:1–8
Psalm 149:1b–2,3–4,5–6a and 9b
Luke 9:7–9

• ST. MICHAEL, ST. GABRIEL, AND ST. RAPHAEL, ARCHANGELS •

I will give thanks to you, O LORD, with all my heart,
for you have heard the words of my mouth;
in the presence of the angels I will sing your praise.
—PSALM 138:1

Today is the feast of three angels—archangels, actually—Michael, Gabriel, and Raphael. They exemplify God's omnipresence, protection, and care. Popular media are fascinated with the idea of angels, depicting them in many movies, television programs, graphic novels, and streaming series. People have an innate sense that there is more to reality than meets the eye, with messengers and protectors hovering around us. Today, we honor the reality of such divinely directed intercessions, inspirations, and interventions in our lives.

Daniel 7:9–10,13–14 or Revelation 12:7–12a
Psalm 138:1–2ab,2cde–3,4–5
John 1:47–51

Saturday

SEPTEMBER 30

• ST. JEROME, PRIEST AND DOCTOR OF THE CHURCH •

Sing and rejoice, O daughter Zion!
See, I am coming to dwell among you, says the LORD.
—ZECHARAIAH 2:14

Human beings struggle to understand how God, so transcendent and so "other," can dwell in our midst, so God has provided many concrete reminders of how close he is: manna in the desert, the Ark of the Covenant, the temple in Jerusalem, and, the greatest of all, the incarnation of his Son, Jesus, in the Eucharist. We can practice the presence of Christ in our daily prayer and meditation, when we receive Holy Communion, and when we take the actions of love to help and serve "the least of these." As the Jesuit poet Gerard Manley Hopkins wrote, "Christ plays in ten thousand places/ Lovely in limbs, and lovely in eyes not his."

Zechariah 2:5–9,14–15a
Jeremiah 31:10,11–12ab,13
Luke 9:43b–45

⋛ 308 ⋚

OCTOBER 1

• TWENTY-SIXTH SUNDAY IN ORDINARY TIME •

A man had two sons.
He came to the first and said,
"Son, go out and work in the vineyard today."
He said in reply, "I will not,"
but afterwards changed his mind and went.
The man came to the other son and gave the same order.
He said in reply, "Yes, sir," but he did not go.
Which of the two did his father's will?
—MATTHEW 21:28–31

Jesus told this parable to nudge the Pharisees into opening their minds. They were so rigidly loyal to what they thought was God's will that they were missing revelations that were happening right in front of their eyes. A dash of humility can help us see that our perceptions of truth may be incomplete.

Ezekiel 18:25–28
Psalm 25:4–5,6–7,8–9 (6a)
Philippians 2:1–11 or 2:1–5
Matthew 21:28–32

Monday

OCTOBER 2

• THE GUARDIAN ANGELS •

*[Jesus said,] "See that you do not despise one of these little ones,
for I say to you that their angels in heaven
always look upon the face of my heavenly Father."*
—MATTHEW 18:10

Today is the feast of the Guardian Angels, messengers of
God assigned to "guard you in all of your ways" (Psalm
91:11). Guardian angels embody the high regard Jesus wants
us to hold for children—all children—because they are
innately deserving of care. Think of all the children you may
encounter in the course of your days. Pray that you can see
them as their guardian angels do—with the image and
likeness of God shining through.

Zechariah 8:1–8
Psalm 102:16–18,19–21,29 and 22–23
Matthew 18:1–5,10

OCTOBER 3

*"Let us go with you, for we have heard that God is
with you."*
—ZECHARIAH 8:23

I have a holy card that I received way back in grammar
school. It was handed out by Sister Edward, my fourth grade
teacher, who gave each one of her students a card as we left
for summer vacation. The card offered suggestions about
having a safe and holy summer, including the wise advice,
"Keep good companions." We are social animals. We will be
influenced by those we hang around. Their interests may
well become our interests. Who are your regular
companions? How are they influencing you? Do their
choices reflect that God is with them?

Zechariah 8:20–23
Psalm 87:1b–3,4–5,6–7
Luke 9:51–56

*W*ednesday

OCTOBER 4

How could we sing a song of the LORD
in a foreign land?
—PSALM 137:4

Sometimes living in the present feels like living in a foreign
land. Life changes so quickly that it's hard to recognize
where we stand. The Jews living in captivity in Babylon
wondered, how could they sing the songs of their faith in
such different circumstances? And yet, how could they not?
Today is the feast of St. Francis of Assisi, who lived in
turbulent and changing times. His experience in battle left
him disoriented, but he prayed. And in prayer he heard Jesus
say, "Repair my church." He did so by returning to the roots
of Christian practice: prayer, poverty, hospitality, simple
living. His example still gives people direction and
hope—and a place to stand.

Nehemiah 2:1–8
Psalm 137:1–2,3,4–5,6
Luke 9:57–62

Thursday

OCTOBER 5

• SAINT FAUSTINA KOWALSKA, VIRGIN • BLESSED FRANCIS XAVIER SEELOS,
PRIEST •

[Jesus said,]
"The harvest is abundant but the laborers are few;
so ask the master of the harvest
to send out laborers for his harvest."
—LUKE 10:2

We all have a calling: to be who God created us to be. What
are you called to be and do? What would change if you
viewed the work you do as a vocation, a calling from God?
Here's a daily practice to help you change your perspective:
whenever you hear yourself say (probably with a bit of
annoyance), "I *have* to do this or that today," reframe it by
saying, "I *get* to do this or that today." Let your day's activities
become blessings rather than burdens.

Nehemiah 8:1–4a,5–6,7b–12
Psalm 19:8,9,10,11
Luke 10:1–12

Friday

OCTOBER 6

Jesus said to them,
"Woe to you, Chorazin! Woe to you, Bethsaida!
For if the mighty deeds done in your midst
had been done in Tyre and Sidon,
they would long ago have repented."
—LUKE 10:13

Jesus faced a good amount of rejection as he traveled the countryside preaching and healing. It must have been frustrating, knowing that what he offered was abundant life in God and yet people still held fast to their old ways. What "old ideas" do I cling to, even when I know they are keeping me from true happiness? How can I grow in willingness to let go of them? Jesus never stopped offering blessings—even from the cross. His offer still stands for you today.

Baruch 1:15–22
Psalm 79:1b–2,3–5,8,9
Luke 10:13–16

Saturday

OCTOBER 7

• OUR LADY OF THE ROSARY •

See, you lowly ones, and be glad;
you who seek God, may your hearts revive!
For the LORD hears the poor,
and his own who are in bonds he spurns not.
—PSALM 69:33–34

One of the appeals of praying the psalms is that they capture both the struggles and the joys people have in their relationship with God. The whole gamut of human emotion shows up. One of the lines that always strikes a chord of consolation in me is "The Lord hears the poor." While I can often feel the gladness of being close to God, there are times when I keenly feel God's absence or, more accurately, my distance from him. Even in that spiritually impoverished state, I am assured that God hears me and responds. What a relief!

Baruch 4:5–12,27–29
Psalm 69:33–35,36–37
Luke 10:17–24

OCTOBER 8

Brothers and sisters:
Have no anxiety at all, but in everything,
by prayer and petition, with thanksgiving,
make your requests known to God.
Then the peace of God that surpasses all understanding
will guard your hearts and minds in Christ Jesus.
—PHILIPPIANS 4:6–7

"Have no anxiety at all . . ." Huh? I don't understand how to do that. Yet, "the peace of God that surpasses all understanding" can be ours. In today's Epistle to the Philippians, St. Paul offers a beautiful recipe for living that can lead to that peace. He says that if we keep our eyes and minds on whatever is true, honorable, just, pure, lovely, gracious, and worthy of praise, "then the God of peace will be with you." Make your requests known to God!

Isaiah 5:1–7
Psalm 80:9,12,13–14,15–16,19–20
Philippians 4:6–9
Matthew 21:33–43

• ST. DENIS, BISHOP, AND COMPANIONS, MARTYRS • ST. JOHN LEONARDI, PRIEST •

But a Samaritan traveler who came upon him
was moved with compassion at the sight.
He approached the victim,
poured oil and wine over his wounds
and bandaged them.
—LUKE 10:33–34

Jesus wanted to dig a little deeper. The scholar in today's reading who approached Jesus surely knew the law, even adding "and your neighbor as yourself" to the command to love God with all you've got. Jesus responded with the familiar story of the priest, Levite, and Samaritan who came upon a wounded man in the road. Who would help? In Jesus' account, the Samaritan, an outsider, didn't see a Jewish person lying there. He saw his neighbor and he acted. Who do I need to add to my perception of who's included when I say the word *us*?

Jonah 1:1—2:2,11
Jonah 2:3,4,5,8
Luke 10:25–37

OCTOBER 10

The Lord said to her in reply,
"Martha, Martha, you are anxious
and worried about many things.
There is need of only one thing."
—LUKE 10:41–42

Here's the reality: a human being can get addicted to just about anything. And being addicted to overwork has the added appeal of getting you lots of praise and providing a handy way to avoid tending to relationships. From what Jesus says to Martha, it appears she has a habit of being anxiously overworked. Usually it starts off positive—because, let's face it, there's a lot to be done in life just to keep up. But then the extra effort becomes the new baseline, and the next, ever higher. But if we get the "one thing" right, which is our relationship with God, we will have an easier time finding the energy and focus to get to the rest, all in due time.

Jonah 3:1–10
Psalm 130:1b–2,3–4ab,7–8
Luke 10:38–42

OCTOBER 11

God said to Jonah,
"Have you reason to be angry over the plant?"
"I have reason to be angry," Jonah answered,
"angry enough to die."
—JONAH 4:9

In the Bible you'll find lofty words of praise and adoration directed at God. And you'll also find gritty conversations like the one above. Imagine this dialogue acted out by James Earl Jones of *Field of Dreams* and Larry David of *Curb Your Enthusiasm* fame. The best description of the conversation would be "blunt." And that was Jonah. I take great comfort in the interactions between God and Jonah. God has endless patience, which is good, because Jonah is endlessly impatient—and impertinent. The lesson I take away is that God has space for my crabby feelings as long as I tell him face-to-face. Holding it in could get you swallowed by a humongous fish.

Jonah 4:1–11
Psalm 86:3–4,5–6,9–10
Luke 11:1–4

OCTOBER 12

[Jesus said,] "For everyone who asks, receives;
and the one who seeks, finds;
and to the one who knocks, the door will be opened."
—LUKE 11:10

I suspect that if we spent a lifetime paying patient attention to all the ways God has blessed us, and specifically to how generously he has responded to our prayers (not necessarily answering them the way we wished but providing for us in ways that prove beneficial in the long run), we would see the evidence behind Jesus' claim that "everyone who asks, receives; and the one who seeks, finds." Doors are opening everywhere if we have the eyes to see and the willingness to walk through them. We might also notice the many times we ask, receive, and fail to acknowledge God's response, thinking we'd handled things so well all on our own.

Malachi 3:13–20b
Psalm 1:1–2,3,4 and 6
Luke 11:5–13

[Jesus said,] "But if it is by the finger of God
that I drive out demons,
then the Kingdom of God has come upon you."
—LUKE 11:20

Critics in the crowd claimed that Jesus cast out demons by the power of Beelzebul, the prince of demons. Jesus questioned their logic: Why would Beelzebul support anyone else bossing around his minions? Beelzebul was all about scattering and causing discord. Jesus came to gather and unite—to promote holy communion between people and with the Father. We can check out our own motives by honestly asking, "Are my actions intended to include and unite? Or would they set one group against another?"

Joel 1:13–15; 2:1–2
Psalm 9:2–3,6 and 16,8–9
Luke 11:15–26

OCTOBER 14

• ST. CALLISTUS I, POPE AND MARTYR •

A woman from the crowd called out and said to him,
"Blessed is the womb that carried you
and the breasts at which you nursed."
[Jesus] replied, "Rather, blessed are those
who hear the word of God and observe it."
—LUKE 11:27–28

People often privilege a prestigious genealogy. The premise is that worth and status flow through birth and even birth order. Jesus was not swayed by accident of birth but rather by the "new birth" that happens when a person hears God's word and takes it to heart and into action. The Blessed Mother has the distinction of being the mother of Jesus, which makes her the mother of God. But her truest and most important status comes from hearing the word of God and saying yes, not just at the Annunciation but throughout her life. Discipleship is more important than any pedigree.

Joel 4:12–21
Psalm 97:1–2,5–6,11–12
Luke 11:27–28

Sunday

OCTOBER 15

• TWENTY-EIGHTH SUNDAY IN ORDINARY TIME •

[Jesus said,] "But when the king came in to meet the guests,
he saw a man there not dressed in a wedding garment.
The king said to him, 'My friend, how is it
that you came in here without a wedding garment?'
But he was reduced to silence."
—MATTHEW 22:11–12

The king in Jesus' parable had trouble with two types of guests: the ones who were invited but failed to attend or even respond, and the ones who seemingly wandered in not dressed for a wedding. The first are the religious leaders who didn't accept Jesus—and many of the prophets before him. The second is the guest dressed for anything but a wedding. Entrance to the feast requires three things: accept the invitation, realize you are part of this marriage, and let the new relationship change your life. Mazel tov!

Isaiah 25:6–10a
Psalm 23:1–3a,3b–4,5,6 (6cd)
Philippians 4:12–14,19–20
Matthew 22:1–14 or 22:1–10

⇒ 323 ⇐

OCTOBER 16

All the ends of the earth have seen
the salvation by our God.
Sing joyfully to the LORD, all you lands;
break into song; sing praise.
—PSALM 98:3–4

Today's psalm verses proclaim that there is no such thing as a godforsaken place. All of creation has seen and speaks convincingly of God's glory. Wherever we go and wherever we are, we can get centered, immersing ourselves in our surroundings, exposed to God's handiwork. In many parts of our country, the changing of the leaves makes this an especially wondrous time to slow down, look around, and appreciate. The seasons have their story to tell, and they all point to God, our creator and source of every good gift.

Romans 1:1–7
Psalm 98:1,2–3ab,3cd–4
Luke 11:29–32

*The Pharisee was amazed to see
that he did not observe the prescribed washing
before the meal.
The Lord said to him, "Oh you Pharisees!
Although you cleanse the outside of the cup
and the dish,
inside you are filled with plunder and evil."*
—LUKE 11:38–39

Jesus found the perfect image to critique the Pharisees' approach to religious practice—polishing the outside of a cup while the inside remains filthy. For Jesus, a living faith requires interior transformation and not mere external actions. What can God and I do today to keep the inside of my cup clean?

Romans 1:16–25
Psalm 19:2–3,4–5
Luke 11:37–41

Your friends make known, O Lord,
the glorious splendor of your Kingdom.
—PSALM 145:12

Today we remember and celebrate the great work of St. Luke, evangelist and traveling companion of St. Paul. Luke wrote a much-beloved Gospel and the follow-up Acts of the Apostles, which chronicles the early days of Christianity, with all its triumphs and challenges. Without the work of Luke, our understanding of Jesus' life and the life of the early church would be greatly diminished. Your life may be the only "Gospel" other people encounter today. Pray that your life will reveal the good news of Jesus and the "glorious splendor" of God's kingdom.

2 Timothy 4:10–17b
Psalm 145:10–11,12–13,17–18
Luke 10:1–9

OCTOBER 19

• ST. JOHN DE BRÉBEUF AND ST. ISAAC JOGUES, PRIESTS, AND COMPANIONS, MARTYRS •

The Lord said,
"Woe to you who build the memorials of the prophets
whom your fathers killed.
Consequently, you bear witness and give consent
to the deeds of your ancestors,
for they killed them and you do the building."
—LUKE 11:47–48

Jesus came with mercy and forgiveness, but first there is judgment, especially for those who already feel righteous and self-satisfied. It's a fine thing to build memorials to the prophets who were murdered, but first there needs to be a moment of culpability. We can't receive forgiveness before we own up to the wrongs we have done. This is not meant to bring shame. Acknowledging our part opens the way to receiving mercy and forgiveness. Claim your wrongdoing so you can hand it over to God.

Romans 3:21–30
Psalm 130:1b–2,3–4,5–6ab
Luke 11:47–54

Friday

OCTOBER 20

• ST. PAUL OF THE CROSS, PRIEST •

*Indeed, if Abraham was justified on the basis
of his works,
he has reason to boast;
but this was not so in the sight of God.*
—ROMANS 4:2–3

A mature spirituality can hold all aspects of a paradox in tension with patience and grace. One major paradox is this question: Are we saved by faith or works? The answer happens to be "both." We cannot be our own saviors, and yet faith without works is dead. Good works done for the right reason strengthen our faith, and commitment to faith leads inexorably to performing good works. Faith, like love, is a mystery we participate in, not a transaction to be performed.

Romans 4:1–8
Psalm 32:1b–2,5,11
Luke 12:1–7

⋛ 328 ⋚

Saturday

OCTOBER 21

[Jesus said,]
*"Everyone who speaks a word against the Son of Man
will be forgiven,
but the one who blasphemes against the Holy Spirit
will not be forgiven."*
—LUKE 12:10

When is a sin unforgivable? When we don't want it to be
forgiven. As Fr. Ronald Rolheiser wrote in his syndicated
column of July 10, 2005, "We commit the sin against the
Holy Spirit when we lie for so long that we believe our own
lies." We become immune to mercy because we lack remorse.
We stubbornly cling to our sin and not to our Savior. That
situation can change in an instant. Recall that when the
prodigal son took a single step back toward home, his father,
who had been waiting in hope for this moment, came
running down the road to welcome him.

Romans 4:13,16–18
Psalm 105:6–7,8–9,42–43
Luke 12:8–12

OCTOBER 22

• TWENTY-NINTH SUNDAY IN ORDINARY TIME •

*The Pharisees went off
and plotted how they might entrap Jesus in speech.*
—MATTHEW 22:15

Threatened by Jesus' growing popularity, the Pharisees posed a simplistic question on a complex topic: "Is it lawful to pay the census tax to Caesar or not?" The question demanded a simplistic answer in reply, one that would pit Jesus against either Rome or the temple leaders. He wasn't fooled by this question that offered false alternatives. Asking the inquirers to show him a coin that pays the census tax (notice that he didn't have one but they did), his answer placed the burden back on them: "Repay to Caesar what belongs to Caesar and to God what belongs to God." When someone with an agenda thrusts a simplistic question on a thorny issue your way, stop and consider, "What would Jesus do?"

Isaiah 45:1,4–6
Psalm 96:1,3,4–5,7–8,9–10 (7b)
1 Thessalonians 1:1–5b
Matthew 22:15–21

OCTOBER 23

• ST. JOHN OF CAPISTRANO, PRIEST •

[The rich man said,]
"I shall tear down my barns and build larger ones.
There I shall store all my grain and other goods
and I shall say to myself, 'Now as for you,
you have so many good things stored up
for many years,
rest, eat, drink, be merry!'"
—LUKE 12:18–19

There was a moment of decision that the farmer blew right by. His harvest was so big that he didn't have space to store it all. "What shall I do?" he asked. And he never thought of another person, not even God. Instead, he decided to tear down his current barns and build larger ones so he could live totally independent. In my decisions today, will I slow down enough to consider what God's will might be or what others might need?

Romans 4:20–25
Luke 1:69–70,71–72,73–75
Luke 12:13–21

OCTOBER 24

• ST. ANTHONY MARY CLARET, BISHOP •

Sacrifice or oblation you wished not,
but ears open to obedience you gave me.
—PSALM 40:7

St. Teresa of Ávila wrote, "All difficulties in prayer can be traced to one cause: praying as if God were absent."[4] We don't need to clamor for God's attention, or, through our goodness, to earn an audience with him. God longs for connection with us. Why else would he give us "ears open to obedience," that is, open to hearing deeply enough to align our will with his? Today, find a quiet time to settle yourself with the knowledge of his presence and pray, "Speak, Lord, your servant is listening," and wait patiently, knowing that no time spent in prayer is wasted.

Romans 5:12,15b,17–19,20b–21
Psalm 40:7–8a,8b–9,10,17
Luke 12:35–38

---

4.   Thomas Keating, *Fruits and Gifts of the Spirit* (New York: Lantern Books, 2000), 1.

Wednesday

OCTOBER 25

But thanks be to God that, although you were once
slaves of sin,
you have become obedient from the heart
to the pattern of teaching to which you
were entrusted.
—ROMANS 6:17

St. Paul can pack a lot into a sentence. Today's passage captures the essence of Paul's preaching. Through God's great goodness we are no longer slaves but free to give ourselves over to "the pattern of teaching to which [we] were entrusted." And what is that pattern of teaching? It is the paschal mystery, that just as Jesus died, we must die to ourselves (i.e., our attachments to sin and the illusion of self-perfection) so we may enjoy new life in God. Today, reflect on ways that new life in Christ is growing in you.

Romans 6:12–18
Psalm 124:1b–3,4–6,7–8
Luke 12:39–48

OCTOBER 26

[Jesus said,]
"Do you think that I have come to establish peace
on the earth?
No, I tell you, but rather division."
—LUKE 12:51

As we close in on the final month of the liturgical year, the Scripture readings become more urgent. Jesus' preaching has been met with acceptance by many and also with rejection and threat by other, very powerful people. Today's passage is not a prediction of what might come but a description of what was already unfolding. Think of it in your own life: When you face a need for significant change in yourself, inner conflict arises, and sometimes outer conflict results as well. We do not need to fear that conflict. When we choose the right path, peace will finally follow.

Romans 6:19–23
Psalm 1:1–2,3,4 and 6
Luke 12:49–53

OCTOBER 27

For I do not do the good I want,
but I do the evil I do not want.
—ROMANS 7:19

St. Paul clearly saw one aspect of the human condition: our tendency to act against our best interests despite our desire to be good and do what is right. I get impatient and snap at my wife. Immediately I regret my action and wonder why it happened yet again. I see an opportunity to get a laugh at someone else's expense and go for it. Immediately after, I get a queasy feeling in my gut and wish I'd bitten my tongue.

"Who will deliver me from this?" asks Paul. His answer? "Thanks be to God through Jesus Christ our Lord." Amen.

Romans 7:18–25a
Psalm 119:66,68,76,77,93,94
Luke 12:54–59

Saturday

OCTOBER 28

• ST. SIMON AND ST. JUDE, APOSTLES •

You are no longer strangers and sojourners,
but you are fellow citizens with the holy ones
and members of the household of God.
—EPHESIANS 2:19

St. Paul's statement that we are members of the household of God strikes a chord of comfort and even relief in me. Who do you turn to when you need support for your spiritual life and growth? Your local parish? A support group with a positive focus? When we say the creed, we don't say, "I believe." It's "We believe," and there's a part of being a follower of Jesus that requires us to attend to the "we" of our faith. Find your "we" and nurture it.

Ephesians 2:19–22
Psalm 19:2–3,4–5
Luke 6:12–16

⇒ 336 ⇐

[A Pharisee asked Jesus,]
"Teacher, which commandment in the law
is the greatest?"
[Jesus] said to him,
"You shall love the Lord, your God,
with all your heart,
with all your soul,
and with all your mind."
—MATTHEW 22:36–37

There were more than six hundred laws to choose from, and the scholar questioning Jesus hoped to trap him by forcing a choice. Jesus stayed out of the weeds and took the big-picture view instead, revealing God's singular purpose behind all the many laws—love. I witnessed the difference when I was tending to my mother before her death. Some days I was doing it out of duty. Other days—the good days—I was there out of love. All I know is that we both enjoyed the latter of the two.

Exodus 22:20–26
Psalm 18:2–3,3–4,47,51 (2)
1 Thessalonians 1:5c–10
Matthew 22:34–40

But the leader of the synagogue,
indignant that Jesus had cured on the sabbath,
said to the crowd in reply,
"There are six days when work should be done.
Come on those days to be cured, not on the sabbath day."
The Lord said to him in reply, "Hypocrites!"
—LUKE 13:14–15

Notice how the leader of the synagogue was indignant at Jesus but yelled at the crowd instead. So he was not only a hypocrite but also a coward. Fully embracing Jesus' radical message can be frightening, and fear often leads to lashing out in all the wrong places. Better we acknowledge the fear and ask God for the strength to overcome its debilitating ways.

Romans 8:12–17
Psalm 68:2 and 4,6–7ab,20–21
Luke 13:10–17

Again [Jesus] said, 'To what shall I compare the
Kingdom of God?
It is like the yeast that a woman took
and mixed in with three measures of wheat flour
until the whole batch of dough was leavened."
—LUKE 13:20–21

The Jews had been invaded by the Roman Empire, which
was merciless and brutal. Jesus proclaimed the coming of the
kingdom of God, which is based on mercy, justice,
compassion, and love. The Romans relied on military might.
Jesus preached a power that was like yeast in the
dough—alive though unseen, transforming, and generating
abundance. Today, think of ways you are like yeast in your
home, parish, workplace, or neighborhood.

Romans 8:18–25
Psalm 126:1b–2ab,2cd–3,4–5,6
Luke 13:18–21

Wednesday

NOVEMBER 1

• ALL SAINTS •

When[Jesus] saw the crowds, he went up the mountain,
and after he had sat down, his disciples came to him.
He began to teach them, saying:
"Blessed are the poor in spirit,
for theirs is the Kingdom of heaven."
—MATTHEW 5:1–3

Jesus saw the crowds. And what did he see? He saw people who were poor, people in mourning, people who remained meek in the face of brutality, people hungry and thirsty for justice, people who were merciful and clean of heart. Maybe they didn't see those things in themselves, but Jesus did, and he called them forth. Many have responded in faith, hope, and love. They are the communion of saints, the "cloud of witnesses" who surround us on our way. As we strive to live our faith, we are not alone. Not by a long shot.

Revelation 7:2–4,9–14
Psalm 24:1b–2,3–4ab,5–6
1 John 3:1–3
Matthew 5:1–12a

NOVEMBER 2

• THE COMMEMORATION OF ALL THE FAITHFUL DEPARTED (ALL SOULS' DAY) •

The souls of the just are in the hand of God,
and no torment shall touch them.
—WISDOM 3:1

Today, Catholics pray for those who have died. Sometimes people we love die, and their lives have been complicated. We may worry that the messiness of their lives excludes them from God's love. We cannot know what has gone on in the hearts of others, but we can be sure of God's boundless mercy and fierce love for each of us. Their souls are in the hand of God, and there's no better place to be.

Wisdom 3:1–9
Romans 5:5–11 or 6:3–9
John 6:37–40
Other readings may be selected.

Friday

NOVEMBER 3

• ST. MARTIN DE PORRES, RELIGIOUS •

*On a sabbath Jesus went to dine
at the home of one of the leading Pharisees,
and the people there were observing him carefully.*
—LUKE 14:1

A large company, hoping to increase worker morale, launched a "We caught you doing something right" program, where individuals could nominate a fellow worker who took action above and beyond the call of duty. At the all-company meeting where they announced it, one of the workers quipped under her breath, "If only we could dismantle the ever-vigorous 'We caught you doing something wrong committee.'" Sometimes we are eager to spread the Good News; sometimes, we're all too ready to delight in the bad. Today, give your attention to what's going well around you, and be ready to say, "Nicely done!"

Romans 9:1–5
Psalm 147:12–13,14–15,19–20
Luke 14:1–6

⋺ 342 ⋹

Blessed the man whom you instruct, O LORD,
whom by your law you teach,
Giving him rest from evil days.
—PSALM 94:12–13A

So how does God instruct us? Author Paula D'Arcy wrote in her spiritual classic *Gift of the Red Bird*, "God comes to us disguised as our life." If we reflect on our lives, we will come to recognize that God speaks to us where we are, as we are. We learn to bring to God even the small hurts and disappointments of our day. We become alert to when fear grips our heart or when we feel an emptiness and want to fill it with activities that fail us. We can bring it all to him—the good, the bad, and the ugly. We'll find that God is surprisingly close and already engaged.

Romans 11:1–2a,11–12,25–29
Psalm 94:12–13a,14–15,17–18
Luke 14:1,7–11

NOVEMBER 5

• THIRTY-FIRST SUNDAY IN ORDINARY TIME •

Have we not all the one father?
Has not the one God created us?
Why then do we break faith with one another,
violating the covenant of our fathers?
—MALACHI 2:10

Why, indeed? We are created in God's image, and God is first and foremost about communion, the unity that encompasses inclusion, mutual forgiveness, and reconciliation. It seems that such peace does not come easily, or naturally. We have to practice peace. Practice inclusion. Practice reconciliation. As St. Mother Teresa often encouraged, we can start in our own homes, neighborhoods, jobs, and parishes. Who do I need to forgive today? To whom do I owe amends? Savor the peace of Christ within you and pass it on.

Malachi 1:14b—2:2b,8–10
Psalm 131:1,2,3
1 Thessalonians 2:7b–9,13
Matthew 23:1–12

[Jesus said,]
"Rather, when you hold a banquet,
invite the poor, the crippled, the lame, the blind;
blessed indeed will you be because of their inability
to repay you."
—LUKE 14:13–14

The Pharisees kept creating more regulations to determine who was in and who was out. Jesus didn't do that; he told stories with a point. As we enter into those stories, we learn from the principle each story reveals. We are then guided by that principle in our thinking, imagining, and acting. In this case, the principle is, be generous without expecting repayment. Take actions without the ulterior motives of looking good, rising in status, or securing a place for ourselves at the next banquet. Be generous today because all good gifts are freely given to us.

Romans 11:29–36
Psalm 69:30–31,33–34,36
Luke 14:12–14

NOVEMBER 7

We, though many, are one Body in Christ
and individually parts of one another.
Since we have gifts that differ according to the grace
given to us,
let us exercise them.
—ROMANS 12:5–6

Our deepest desire is communion; our base instinct is
competition. No wonder we are at war with ourselves—and
often with each other. We don't see the world as it is; we see
the world as we are, which tends toward comparison and
competition. Jesus offers an antidote to the splintered and
defensive ways we can see the world, but it doesn't come easy.
We have to "put on the mind of Christ," which means we need
to see others as neighbors and all of us as one body in him. Try
this: If you find yourself feeling at odds with someone today,
imagine how Jesus sees that person. Does he see more than you
currently do? Are you open to seeing that too?

Romans 12:5–16b
Psalm 131:1bcde,2,3
Luke 14:15–24

Love does no evil to the neighbor;
hence, love is the fulfillment of the law.
—ROMANS 13:10

Life can be messy, complicated, and perplexing. Perhaps you're experiencing some of that now: a confusing relationship, an argumentative coworker, a child in your life who seems in distress and won't tell you why, or even a feeling that God is on sabbatical and unreachable. No matter how confused and uncertain you may be, there is one bedrock response you can always rely on: do the next loving thing in front of you. Perhaps those thorny situations cannot be improved right now—but there's always someone nearby who could benefit from your loving action. Take the action you can, and trust the Holy Spirit to work on the rest.

Romans 13:8–10
Psalm 112:1b–2,4–5,9
Luke 14:25–33

Thursday

NOVEMBER 9

• THE DEDICATION OF THE LATERAN BASILICA •

Do you not know that you are the temple of God,
and that the Spirit of God dwells in you?
—1 CORINTHIANS 3:16

In today's first reading, Ezekiel tells of a vision where water flowed out from the temple into barren lands, bringing forth trees of every kind that bear abundant fruit for food and leaves for medicine. This seems like a good description of what a good local parish can do—pour out new life into the surrounding neighborhoods to nurture and to heal. And then St. Paul makes the astonishing claim that *we* are the temple of God, and wherever we go, we bear the Spirit of God to that place. Images like these help us see what's possible if we are willing to be temples of the Holy Spirit and channels of grace.

Ezekiel 47:1–2,8–9,12
Psalm 46:2–3,5–6,8–9
1 Corinthians 3:9c–11,16–17
John 2:13–22

NOVEMBER 10

• ST. LEO THE GREAT, POPE AND DOCTOR OF THE CHURCH •

Sing joyfully to the LORD, all you lands;
break into song; sing praise.
—PSALM 98:4

One of my favorite memories is returning from church with our two young daughters and hearing them spontaneously sing one or more of the hymns we'd heard at Mass. Other times I'd hear them singing or humming a hymn during the week while they were playing with their toys or coloring. It was gratifying to know that those words—"Gather us in," "Be not afraid," "Let us build the city of God"—were in their minds and hearts, and not just the words of songs they'd hear on the radio. With music streaming services so available, you can easily add some of your favorite hymns to your playlist and make them the soundtrack of your life.

Romans 15:14–21
Psalm 98:1,2–3ab,3cd–4
Luke 16:1–8

NOVEMBER 11

• ST. MARTIN OF TOURS, BISHOP •

*Greet Prisca and Aquila, my co-workers in Christ Jesus,
who risked their necks for my life,
to whom not only I am grateful but also all the
churches of the Gentiles.*
—ROMANS 16:3–4

In the final chapter of St. Paul's letter to the Romans, he introduces his readers to more than two dozen people, men and women who were actively involved in building up local churches in the early days of Christianity. Reading their names—Mary, Andronicus, Junia, Ampliatus, Stachys, etc.—makes that time in the church seem very real. I could call out the names Roy, Betty, Chris, Dave, Ruth, Hector, Mario and Yanira, etc.—people in my own parish who keep the work of Christ alive in our day. We are part of a long tradition. Remember the past; work for the future.

Romans 16:3–9,16,22–27
Psalm 145:2–3,4–5,10–11
Luke 16:9–15

> [Jesus said,]
> *"The kingdom of heaven will be like ten virgins*
> *who took their lamps and went out to meet*
> *the bridegroom.*
> *Five of them were foolish and five were wise.*
> *The foolish ones, when taking their lamps,*
> *brought no oil with them."*
> —MATTHEW 25:1–3

Have you ever dreamt that you arrive at school for a final test and realize you never attended a single class? I cringe even writing that line. Well, that's how the foolish virgins must have felt when the bridegroom arrived in the dead of night. In the spiritual life, we cannot do all our homework the night before the final. To properly prepare, we must do the work of coming to know, love, and serve God every day of our lives. Then our lamps will shine bright.

Wisdom 6:12–16
Psalm 63:2,3–4,5–6,7–8 (2b)
1 Thessalonians 4:13–18 or 4:13–14
Matthew 25:1–13

O LORD, you have probed me and you know me;
you know when I sit and when I stand;
you understand my thoughts from afar.
—PSALM 139:1–2

As a kid I used to be terrified that God could see everything I did. But now I've come to believe that, at some level, most people want to be seen, known, and blessed. Try this out: Sit in a quiet place with an empty chair or sofa across from you. Quiet your mind as best you can. Imagine that Jesus is sitting across from you. Tell him what's going on in your heart right now. Can you imagine him smiling kindly at you? Say all that you want to say, or sit quietly together. Thank him for the time you have shared.

Wisdom 1:1–7
Psalm 139:1b–3,4–6,7–8,9–10
Luke 17:1–6

Tuesday

NOVEMBER 14

I will bless the LORD at all times,
his praise shall be ever in my mouth.
—PSALM 34:2

I would like to claim this is true for me—that I will bless the
Lord at all times—but I cannot. There are times when I argue
with God or just plain yell at him. Worse, I sometimes forget
him. And there are psalms I can go to that will capture my
feelings at those times. But this goal is something I aspire to,
because it would mean that I am thinking with the mind of
Jesus, who even in his own agony and death remained
attuned with and united to the Father. If I want to bless the
Lord at all times, I need to follow St. Paul's advice to "pray
always," even if my prayers come out as rants. Those, too,
can quickly turn to praise.

Wisdom 2:23—3:9
Psalm 34:2–3,16–17,18–19
Luke 17:7–10

As Jesus continued his journey to Jerusalem,
he traveled through Samaria and Galilee.
As he was entering a village, ten lepers met him.
They stood at a distance from him.

—LUKE 17:11–12

The ones suffering with leprosy stood at a distance from Jesus—and from everyone but one another. That was their plight. They were exiled from the community. There are many ways people are exiled—outward appearance, financial status, mental illness, age, social awkwardness. Often people learn to self-exile because they've been hurt too often. Maybe you've experienced such shunning yourself. Jesus came so that we all may be one. Today, make an effort to see others as Jesus saw everyone he met—as precious and beloved daughters and sons of God.

Wisdom 6:1–11
Psalm 82:3–4,6–7
Luke 17:11–19

NOVEMBER 16

• ST. MARGARET OF SCOTLAND • ST. GERTRUDE THE GREAT, VIRGIN •

For she is the refulgence of eternal light,
the spotless mirror of the power of God,
the image of his goodness.
—WISDOM: 7:26

Today's Scripture passage is from the book of Wisdom, written about fifty years before the coming of Christ. The book focuses on the splendor and value of divine wisdom as a quality to avidly pursue. The author says of wisdom, "Passing into holy souls from age to age, she produces friends of God and prophets." Acquaint yourself with wisdom by spending time in receptive silence, contemplating God's handiwork, and allowing her to pass into your soul and guide you with the radiance of eternal light.

Wisdom 7:22b–8:1
Psalm 119:89,90,91,130,135,175
Luke 17:20–25

[Jesus said,] "As it was in the days of Noah,
so it will be in the days of the Son of Man;
they were eating and drinking,
marrying and giving in marriage up to the day
that Noah entered the ark,
and the flood came and destroyed them all."
—LUKE 17:26–29

As we approach the end of the liturgical year, many of the readings speak of the "end times." Today's reading reflects how Jesus is moving deliberately toward Jerusalem, knowing he faces danger, even death. We can use these readings as an opportunity to take stock of who we are and where we are heading. Life is not a series of random events with no meaning or purpose. God is our source and our destiny, and our task is to deepen our life in him, no matter what is happening around us.

Wisdom 13:1–9
Psalm 19:2–3,4–5ab
Luke 17:26–37

NOVEMBER 18

• THE DEDICATION OF THE BASILICA OF ST. PETER AND ST. PAUL, APOSTLES
• ST. ROSE PHILIPPINE DUCHESNE, VIRGIN •

Peter got out of the boat and began to walk
on the water toward Jesus.
But when he saw how strong the wind was
he became frightened;
and, beginning to sink, he cried out, "Lord, save me!"
Immediately Jesus stretched out his hand
and caught him.
—MATTHEW 14:29–31

I've never walked on water, but there are times when I get
way out ahead of my skis and, like Peter, become frightened.
Today's passage is a lesson in the dynamics of faith and fear:
more fear/less faith; more faith/less fear. Peter may have been
too sure of himself when he clambered out of the boat and
began to walk, but he knew what to do when that sinking
feeling of fear came over him: cry out to the Lord for help.

Wisdom 18:14–16; 19:6–9 or Acts 28:11–16,30–31
Psalm 105:2–3,36–37,42–43 or 98:1,2–3ab,3cd–4,5–6
Luke 18:1–8 or Matthew 14:22–33

NOVEMBER 19

• THIRTY-THIRD SUNDAY IN ORDINARY TIME •

*[Jesus said,] "Immediately the one who received five talents
went and traded with them
and made another five.
Likewise, the one who received two made another two.
But the man who received one went off and dug a hole
in the ground
and buried his master's money."*
—MATTHEW 25:15–18

Jesus expects us to take our gifts and talents and use them to
further the kingdom. We are responsible for what we make of
our unique talents, whether it's inventing a cure for cancer or
making a child feel welcome on the first day of school. We
need to respond with the unique talents we have. We can't
just bury our gifts as if they don't exist. Do you recognize
and appreciate your unique gifts? How do you answer Jesus'
call to make the most of them?

Proverbs 31:10–13,19–20,30–31
Psalm 128:1–2,3,4–5
1 Thessalonians 5:1–6
Matthew 25:14–30 or 25:14–15,19–21

Jesus asked him,
"What do you want me to do for you?"
He replied, "Lord, please let me see."
—LUKE 18:40–41

Today's Gospel reading is about being healed on two levels.
Jesus sees the blind man who cries out to him, hoping to be
seen. Jesus sees not only the man's outer appearance but also
what his soul is lacking. How well do I recognize not only
my immediate physical needs but also what I lack spiritually?
Is it faith, trust, willingness to change, courage to see or act?
The physical and spiritual are often intertwined, and I can
ask God to heal both. "Lord, please let me see!"

1 Maccabees 1:10–15,41–43,54–57,62–63
Psalm 119:53,61,134,150,155,158
Luke 18:35–43

But Zacchaeus stood there and said to the Lord,
"Behold, half of my possessions, Lord,
I shall give to the poor,
and if I have extorted anything from anyone
I shall repay it four times over."
—LUKE 19:8

Real conversion changes everything: body, mind, heart, and behavior. Zacchaeus shows it's not enough to say we're sorry; we also have to make things right for those we've harmed. Owning up to his previous life of corruption, Zacchaeus agrees to give half his wealth to the poor and repay fourfold those he had cheated. True conversion requires not just forgiveness but also restoration and reconciliation. Is there an outstanding amends I need to make? God, give me the grace and strength to make things right where I ought.

2 Maccabees 6:18–31
Psalm 3:2–3,4–5,6–7
Luke 19:1–10

NOVEMBER 22

"I will not obey the king's command.
I obey the command of the law given to our fathers
through Moses."
—2 MACCABEES 7:30

The books of Maccabees 1 and 2 tell the story of Jewish persecution that happened about two hundred years before Jesus. The king at that time allied with certain gentile groups and outlawed every vestige of Jewish religious practice. The story quoted here tells of a mother and her seven sons who were tortured for refusing to engage in pagan practices. All seven sons were killed, and these are the words of the youngest son right before his death. This reading invites us to pray for and do what we can to support the many people around the world still suffering for their faith.

2 Maccabees 7:1,20–31
Psalm 17:1bcd,5–6,8b and 15
Luke 19:11–28

NOVEMBER 23

> *I give thanks to my God always on your account*
> *for the grace of God bestowed on you in Christ Jesus,*
> *that in turn you were enriched in every way.*
> —1 CORINTHIANS 1:4–5

St. Paul was obviously deeply invested in the spiritual welfare of those he brought to faith in Jesus. His letters to the churches he founded are full of passionate care and concern. On this Thanksgiving holiday we focus our attention on all our blessings, including the people in our lives we love and care about. Today, make time to reflect on the many people who have enriched your life with their presence and their care. Cast the net widely, including people from your past who made a significant difference in your life.

1 Maccabees 2:15–29
Psalm 50:1b–2,5–6,14–15
Luke 19:41–44

For Thanksgiving Day, any readings from
the Mass "In Thanksgiving to God"

*Jesus entered the temple area and proceeded to drive out
those who were selling things, saying to them,
"It is written, My house shall be a house of prayer,
but you have made it a den of thieves."*
—LUKE 19:45–46

Though the Pharisees were critical of tax collectors who used
their power to extort, they failed to see that they did the
same thing. Believers were expected to offer animals for
sacrifice, which, conveniently, they could purchase on
temple grounds. Jesus was furious that they were squeezing
the people and also supporting a false notion of God—that
we have to buy God's favor rather than simply offer our
"humble and contrite hearts." The rift between Jesus and the
religious leaders has now hit a point of no return. Ask, do I
believe I have to earn God's attention?

1 Maccabees 4:36–37,52–59
1 Chronicles 29:10bcd,11abc,11d–12a,12bcd
Luke 19:45–48

NOVEMBER 25

• ST. CATHERINE OF ALEXANDRIA, VIRGIN AND MARTYR •

I will give thanks to you, O LORD, with all my heart;
I will declare all your wondrous deeds.
—PSALM 9:2

Last Thursday (Thanksgiving) you might have sung, "Now thank we all our God, with hearts and hands and voices." Think of ways you can express your gratitude with your heart, your hands, and your voice in the next few days. Using your heart, make a gratitude list. With your hands, do something nice for someone you are grateful for. And with your voice, talk to (in person or by phone, text, email) someone you are grateful for and let them know. May this set a tone for the days of preparation and celebration just ahead.

1 Maccabees 6:1–13
Psalm 9:2–3,4 and 6,16 and 19
Luke 20:27–40

NOVEMBER 26

• OUR LORD JESUS CHRIST, KING OF THE UNIVERSE •

*[Jesus said,] "The righteous will answer [the Son of Man] and say,
'Lord, when did we see you hungry and feed you,
or thirsty and give you drink?
When did we see you a stranger and welcome you,
or naked and clothe you?'"*
—MATTHEW 25:37–38

Today's reading, the final Sunday of the liturgical year,
features the king separating the sheep and the goats.
Theologian John Shea suggests three qualities of the "sheep."
They were (1) *proactive* (not engaging in an internal
monologue about the merits of acting or not); (2)
uncalculating (not considering whether the recipient was
deserving or could reciprocate); and (3) *unobtrusive* (acting
freely and expecting no credit for what they did). In other
words, they simply acted whenever they saw a need, without
asking "what's in it for me," and it was no big deal. Let your
goodness flow.

Ezekiel 34:11–12,15–17
Psalm 23:1–2,2–3,5–6 (1)
1 Corinthians 15:20–26,28
Matthew 25:31–46

When Jesus looked up he saw some wealthy people
putting their offerings into the treasury
and he noticed a poor widow putting in
two small coins.
—LUKE 21:1–2

Our goal as Christians is to become more and more like Jesus. Today's reading gives us an insight into an essential quality of Jesus—empathy. He saw things. He saw the rich making their donations, and he saw the widow doing the same. But his empathy allowed him to see what made it not the same—the relative cost to each person of making their donation. Jesus had both the vision to see others and a deep empathy for what was going on inside them. The capacity for empathy is the gateway to all morality. Today, practice viewing people with empathy rather than with judgment.

Daniel 1:1–6,8–20
Daniel 3:52,53,54,55,56
Luke 21:1–4

Tuesday

NOVEMBER 28

*"In the lifetime of those kings
the God of heaven will set up a kingdom
that shall never be destroyed or delivered up
to another people;
rather, it shall break in pieces all these kingdoms
and put an end to them, and it shall stand forever."*
—DANIEL 2:44

God gave Daniel the gift of interpreting dreams. He was
called upon by both King Nebuchadnezzar and his son
Belshazzar to interpret their dreams, and the news wasn't
good for either one. Today's reading speaks of a new
kingdom being established by God that will overthrow the
current unjust kingdoms, including Nebuchadnezzar's own.
Sidenote: Testifying to the staying power of Daniel's
prophesying, we get the phrases "feet of clay" and "reading
the handwriting on the wall" from the vivid imagery in his
dream interpretations.

Daniel 2:31–45
Daniel 3:57,58,59,60,61
Luke 21:5–11

NOVEMBER 29

*"Sun and moon, bless the Lord;
praise and exalt him above all forever.
Stars of heaven, bless the Lord;
praise and exalt him above all forever."*
—DANIEL 3:62–63

The book of Daniel was created from various traditional
stories and prayers that tell of the trials and triumphs of
Daniel, a wise and faithful Jew, and his three companions.
Daniel, not the author of the book but its hero, lived around
500 BC during the Babylonian exile, but the stories were
gathered in one source around 167–164 BC, during the bitter
persecution under Antiochus IV, in hopes that Daniel's
example would provide strength and comfort to the Jewish
people in their ordeal. In the midst of that cruelty, a long and
beautiful prayer is inserted, affirming the goodness of God
and his many blessings to us.

Daniel 5:1–6,13–14,16–17,23–28
Daniel 3:62,63,64,65,66,67
Luke 21:12–19

NOVEMBER 30

• ST. ANDREW, APOSTLE •

As Jesus was walking by the sea of Galilee,
he saw two brothers,
Simon, who is called Peter, and his brother Andrew,
casting a net into the sea.
—MATTHEW 4:18

Andrew was a fisherman and early follower of John the Baptist. Andrew was the one who first told his brother Peter about Jesus. Despite his being the first apostle, we do not hear much more about Andrew in the Gospel. We do know that he continued talking about Jesus long after Pentecost. Many of us can relate to Andrew—just one of the team who reliably got the message out and the work done. And when he faced death by crucifixion, Andrew humbly asked that his cross be in the shape of an X so he would not be equating himself to his Lord, Jesus.

Romans 10:9–18
Psalm 19:8,9,10,11
Matthew 4:18–22

*In a vision, I, Daniel, saw during the night,
the four winds of heaven stirred up the great sea,
from which emerged four immense beasts.*
—DANIEL 7:2–3

The book of Daniel is an example of apocalyptic literature, a
fabricated story that reflects and reveals a current truth. The
most important thing to know about apocalyptic writing is
that it is too important to take literally. People tend to look
for certainty in the midst of trouble, and so they scour
ancient writings for predictions. The apocalyptic literature
found among the accepted books of the Bible all contains a
hopeful message: No matter what comes, God's love will
prevail. As a Scripture professor once told us, the core
message is, "Tough times don't last; faithful people do."

Daniel 7:2–14
Daniel 3:75,76,77,78,79,80,81
Luke 21:29–33

DECEMBER 2

*Beware that your hearts do not become drowsy
from carousing and drunkenness
and the anxieties of daily life,
and that day catch you by surprise like a trap.*
—LUKE 21:34–35

Life is a series of endings and new beginnings. Sometimes the endings can be quite demanding. On this, the last day of the liturgical year and the eve of Advent, the church places Jesus' warning to his disciples: "Do not become drowsy!" In troubling times, we are prone to escape, to hide our heads in the sand, or as social commentator Neil Postman put it, amuse ourselves to death. It takes courage, faith, and hope to face the fears that accompany living. Tomorrow, we once again begin preparing our hearts for the coming of Jesus, and the story of hope, healing, and salvation begins anew.

Daniel 7:15–27
Daniel 3:82,83,84,85,86,87
Luke 21:34–36

Yet, O LORD, you are our father;
we are the clay and you the potter:
we are all the work of your hands.
—ISAIAH 64:7

We begin Advent and the new liturgical year with a powerful
image of our relationship to God. We see not an aloof deity
floating high in remote heavenly regions. Instead, we see a
God who is a father, whose hands have formed us, and whose
breath gives us life. Spend time today checking in on your
image of God. Ask yourself, *Who is God to me? And who am I*
to God?

Isaiah 63:16b–17,19b; 64:2–7
Psalm 80:2–3,15–16,18–19 (4)
1 Corinthians 1:3–9
Mark 13:33–37

DECEMBER 4

• ST. JOHN DAMASCENE, PRIEST AND DOCTOR OF THE CHURCH •

"Come let us climb the LORD's mountain,
to the house of the God of Jacob,
That he may instruct us in his ways,
and we may walk in his paths."

—ISAIAH 2:3

In Advent we get in touch with our deeper longings, and the deepest longing, placed within us by God, is to see him more clearly, love him more dearly, and follow him more nearly. So the image of climbing a mountain is a good way to engage our imaginations. Climbing to high places requires that we take our time and pay attention to each step. It offers times of rest to look around and see our lives from a new, wider perspective. In the stillness, we can listen for the voice of God. Commit to making time each day to give yourself to this journey.

Isaiah 2:1–5
Psalm 122:1–2,3–4b,4cd–5,6–7,8–9
Matthew 8:5–11

DECEMBER 5

The Spirit of the LORD shall rest upon him:
a Spirit of wisdom and of understanding,
A Spirit of counsel and of strength,
a Spirit of knowledge and of fear of the LORD.
—ISAIAH 11:2

I was talking to a friend about an upcoming parish meeting. I was worried about how the meeting would go, and whether certain people's animosity would be on display. He stopped me and asked, "So, what spirit do you want to be in when you arrive there?" His question called forth the grace I needed in that situation. Instead of scanning the horizon for problems, I could ask God's help to immerse myself in the Spirit of wisdom and understanding. Come, Lord Jesus!

Isaiah 11:1–10
Psalm 72:1–2,7–8,12–13,17
Luke 10:21–24

The LORD is my shepherd, I shall not want.
In verdant pastures he gives me repose;
Beside restful waters he leads me;
he refreshes my soul.
—PSALM 23:1–3

Advent gives us time to rest. It offers time to lift our heads up from the daily concerns that can absorb all our energy and focus. Today's readings speak of experiences of abundance where scarcity is feared. Today, recall a time when you experienced surprising abundance—a family gathering, a holiday feast, a surprise visit with a friend. Sit in the glow of that memory and express your gratitude to God.

Isaiah 25:6–10a
Psalm 23:1–3a,3b–4,5,6
Matthew 15:29–37

DECEMBER 7

• ST. AMBROSE, BISHOP AND DOCTOR OF THE CHURCH •

Jesus said to his disciples:
"Not everyone who says to me, 'Lord, Lord,'
will enter the Kingdom of heaven,
but only the one who does the will
of my Father in heaven."
—MATTHEW 7:21

One of the challenges of being a follower of Jesus is that we leave ourselves open to judgment about whether we not only talk the talk but also walk the walk. Jesus invites us, "Follow me." It's not "admire me," or "earn my good graces," or even, "proclaim me." The will of the Father is that we love one another, in deed as well as intention or speech. Gently check in on your behavior the past twenty-four hours. Ask yourself, Where did my actions show that I was following Jesus? What can I do today to treat others as Jesus would?

Isaiah 26:1–6
Psalm 118:1 and 8–9,19–21,25–27a
Matthew 7:21,24–27

Mary said, "Behold, I am the handmaid of the Lord.
May it be done to me according to your word."
—LUKE 1:38

Like bookends, Mary's yes to the angel prefigures Jesus'
words of assent to his Father during his agony in the garden.
The Blessed Mother's, "May it be done to me according to
your word" and Jesus', "Not my will, but yours be done"
reveal that alignment with God's will is essential to both the
promise and fulfillment of Jesus' mission on earth. After
contemplating Mary's and Jesus' liberating acts of faith and
surrender, pray, "God, help me to know and embrace your
will for me."

Genesis 3:9–15,20
Psalm 98:1,2–3ab,3cd–4
Ephesians 1:3–6,11–12
Luke 1:26–38

At the sight of the crowds, his heart was moved with
pity for them
because they were troubled and abandoned,
like sheep without a shepherd.
—MATTHEW 9:36

Troubled and abandoned. That's what Jesus saw in the faces of the people who sought him out and hung on his every word. His first move was compassion, and healing closely followed. When we feel lost, we may be tempted to escape those feelings in all the wrong ways: binge-watching, overeating, compulsive shopping, living in fantasy or lust, any of the seven deadly sins. The truth is that you can never get enough of that which cannot satisfy. Jesus invites people to abandon those fruitless ways and find fullness and joy by making a real connection with God.

Isaiah 30:19–21,23–26
Psalm 147:1–2,3–4,5–6
Matthew 9:35—10:1,5a,6–8

Sunday

DECEMBER 10

• SECOND SUNDAY OF ADVENT •

Kindness and truth shall meet;
justice and peace shall kiss.
Truth shall spring out of the earth,
and justice shall look down from heaven.
—PSALM 85:11–12

Kindness is powerful. It can totally transform a situation or a person. To receive an act of kindness can lead to a reawakening to hope. To perform an act of kindness can feel like redemption. Heading into your day with the intention of kindness is a powerful way to make real the spirit of Advent. In kindness, we prepare the way of the Lord.

Isaiah 40:1–5,9–11
Psalm 85:9–10,11–12,13–14 (8)
2 Peter 3:8–14
Mark 1:1–8

⇒ 379 ⇐

And some men brought on a stretcher a man who
was paralyzed;
they were trying to bring him in and set him
in his presence.
—LUKE 5:18

Just putting ourselves in Jesus' presence is powerful. Consider the paralyzed man and the love of his friends that moved them to bring him before Jesus. In his encounter with Jesus, the man who had been paralyzed experienced healing on many levels—not least of which was being able to walk and being restored to life in the community. Can you think of a time when being with your friends became an occasion of encountering Jesus and experiencing healing? Pray a prayer of thanksgiving for those friends.

Isaiah 35:1–10
Psalm 85:9ab and 10,11–12,13–14
Luke 5:17–26

Tuesday

DECEMBER 12

• OUR LADY OF GUADALUPE •

Your deed of hope will never be forgotten
by those who tell of the might of God.
—JUDITH 13:19

It's appropriate that Our Lady of Guadalupe appeared to Juan Diego as pregnant, because she was bearing Jesus to people facing radical change. The people who had lived for ages in what we now call Central America had just had their lives and sense of reality disrupted. Mary's presence communicated a mother's love and the promise of accompaniment. Our Lady of Guadalupe shines for all of us today as a sign of hope and courage. Change continues to impact us all. She reminds us that in every moment, however difficult, Christ lives.

Zechariah 2:14–17 or Revelation 11:19a; 12:1–6a,10ab
Judith 13:18bcde,19
Luke 1:26–38 or 1:39–47

⇒ 381 ⇐

Wednesday

DECEMBER 13

• ST. LUCY, VIRGIN AND MARTYR •

He pardons all your iniquities,
he heals all your ills.
He redeems your life from destruction,
he crowns you with kindness and compassion.
—PSALM 103:3–4

During Advent, we recognize our longing to grow closer to
God. But we also need to recognize what keeps us away.
Sometimes unreconciled sins and failures keep us from
accepting God's invitation. We may not feel worthy of
approaching the child in the manger. We can pray for the
grace to accept God's invitation to draw closer and the grace to
accept God's forgiveness of what we have done and what we
have failed to do. We are not perfect, but we are alive. And
God's will is that we enter more deeply into life. Be not afraid.

Isaiah 40:25–31
Psalm 103:1–2, 3–4, 8 and 10
Matthew 11:28–30

Thursday

DECEMBER 14

The afflicted and the needy seek water in vain,
their tongues are parched with thirst.
I, the Lord will answer them:
I the God of Israel, will not forsake them.
I will open up rivers on the bare heights,
and fountains in the broad valleys.
—ISAIAH 41:17–18

Water is a rich and powerful symbol with a variety of associations. One of the most powerful is how water symbolizes God's own life and grace. Meditate a while on today's passage from Isaiah. Is there dryness in your spiritual life right now? Imagine the drought. Feel it. Then imagine God opening up rivers on the bare heights and fountains in the broad valleys. See the sun glistening on the swirling rivers; hear the splashing of the water as it overflows into the valley. Accept the grace of new life bubbling up in you.

Isaiah 41:13–20
Psalm 145:1 and 9,10–11,12–13ab
Matthew 11:11–15

*I, the LORD, your God,
teach you what is for your good,
and lead you on the way you should go.*
—ISAIAH 48:17

Yesterday I saw a mom and her young daughter having a disagreement as they got into their car. Just before the door slammed, the daughter yelled, "You just don't want me to have any fun!" I've had that same conversation with God: "You just don't want me to have any fun!" It takes a bit of growing up to accept that God's purpose doesn't stop at *Thou shalt not*. We need also consider the "so that" portion of the equation. God says, "Don't sin *so that* you can avoid misery, be a better person, and have better relationships—including with me." God's ways happen to be the way to satisfaction, fulfillment, and joy.

Isaiah 48:17–19
Psalm 1:1–2,3,4 and 6
Matthew 11:16–19

DECEMBER 16

*As they were coming down from the mountain,
the disciples asked Jesus,
"Why do the scribes say that Elijah must come first?"*
—MATTHEW 17:9A–10

People kept waiting for the return of Elijah, "whose words were as a flaming furnace" (Sirach 48:1). I suspect many of them expected Elijah would do for them what they could not or would not do for themselves—scare them into repenting and turning their lives wholly over to God. Jesus reminded them that John the Baptist, who followed in Elijah's fiery footsteps, had come and the religious and civil authorities "did to him whatever they pleased." No, Jesus would blaze a new path. He would preach justice, forgiveness, and compassion. He would suffer and die but be raised from the dead to show us the path we must follow to new and eternal life.

Sirach 48:1–4,9–11
Psalm 80:2ac and 3b,15–16,18–19
Matthew 17:9a,10–13

The spirit of the Lord GOD is upon me,
because the LORD has anointed me;
he has sent me to bring glad tidings to the poor,
to heal the brokenhearted,
to proclaim liberty to the captives
and release to the prisoners.
—ISAIAH 61:1

These words of Isaiah not only point to Jesus but also manage to capture the essence of who he was and what mattered most to him. Jesus was deeply attuned to the spirit of the Lord God. He was immersed in it, guided by it, and everything he did or said was inspired by that spirit. This is the spirit that is moved by compassion for the poor and the brokenhearted, who frees prisoners and calls forth the favor of the Lord. The Holy Spirit of God is at work in the world, at work in you. Lean into it.

Isaiah 61:1–2a,10–11
Luke 1:46–48,49–50,53–54
1 Thessalonians 5:16–24
John 1:6–8,19–28

Behold, the days are coming, says the LORD,
When I will raise up a righteous shoot to David.
—JEREMIAH 23:5

Early in these reflections we learned to be alert whenever the
word *behold* was used in the text. Its appearance signals that
God is about to be made manifest in the words or actions
that come next. During Advent we should put up a sign in a
prominent place that reminds us to "behold," because what
we are preparing to celebrate is the most significant action of
God since he declared into the void, "Let there be light!"
Look for signs of Jesus' coming: justice prevailing, kindnesses
shown, songs of joy and hope, generosity welling up and
overflowing. 'Tis the season to behold!

Jeremiah 23:5–8
Psalm 72:1–2,12–13,18–19
Matthew 1:18–25

DECEMBER 19

You are my hope, O LORD;
my trust, O God from my youth.
On you I depend from birth;
from my mother's womb you are my strength.
—PSALM 71:5–6AB

Advent is a time for memories. Take time today to recall favorite memories of preparing for Christmas when you were young: favorite movies or TV Christmas specials, favorite customs, decorations, Christmas lights, visits with friends and relatives, midnight Mass, Christmas carols, waiting in joyful hope. Let those memories fill you. Let your grateful heart overflow.

Judges 13:2–7,24–25a
Psalm 71:3–4a,5–6ab,16–17
Luke 1:5–25

DECEMBER 20

Therefore the Lord himself will give you this sign:
the virgin shall conceive and bear a son,
and shall name him Emmanuel.
—ISAIAH 7:14

Let's continue our theme of memory, which seems to come naturally in the run-up to Christmas. Take time today to recall moments when you felt God's presence in your midst. I can recall visits with cousins and aunts and uncles, going caroling up and down our block, and praying before the elaborate and mysterious manger scene in our parish church as I imagined being present on the day Jesus was born. You can cultivate your awareness of God's presence by reflecting at the end of each day and noticing the times when you felt God was close. You may be surprised at what you've been missing.

Isaiah 7:10–14
Psalm 24:1–2,3–4ab,5–6
Luke 1:26–38

Thursday

DECEMBER 21

On that day, it shall be said to Jerusalem:
Fear not, O Zion, be not discouraged!
The LORD, your God, is in your midst,
a mighty savior.
—ZEPHANIAH 3:16–17

Many people find the Christmas season to be an emotionally difficult time. They get discouraged that they aren't feeling particularly jolly. Over the course of our lives, we will feel many different ways during the Advent/Christmas seasons. The reality of Christmas goes far deeper than our transitory feelings. So, fear not if you aren't feeling merry or bright. Take comfort that the Lord God is in our midst and he is here to save us.

Song of Songs 2:8–14 or Zephaniah 3:14–18a
Psalm 33:2–3,11–12,20–21
Luke 1:39–45

Mary said:
"My soul proclaims the greatness of the Lord,
my spirit rejoices in God my savior,
for he has looked upon his lowly servant."
—LUKE 1:46–47

Mary reveals what happens when a person experiences a profound encounter with God. First, you become acutely aware of God's majesty and power, and you feel small. Second, you experience deep-down blessing, and your heart expands so that you can't help but proclaim the greatness of God. In that encounter, our egos become right-sized; we know we are not everything but that we are, indeed, persons of value who bear the image of God. Not having to manufacture our own self-worth, we can let God be God and become our true selves, the precious ones that God created. Pay attention. God looks upon you, too.

1 Samuel 1:24–28
1 Samuel 2:1,4–5,6–7,8abcd
Luke 1:46–56

Thus says the Lord GOD
Lo, I am sending my messenger
to prepare the way before me;
And suddenly there will come to the temple
the LORD whom you seek.
—MALACHI 3:1

During Advent we have been preparing by turning our hearts away from distractions and poor substitutes (aka looking for satisfaction in all the wrong places, like endless hours on social media, overeating, compulsive shopping, feeding our resentments, indulging our fears, etc.). As we approach the celebration of Christmas, the church has chosen readings that once again ring out the call to prepare. It's never too late to have a good Advent. What's standing in the way of your approaching the Christ child? Let it go. Now. Become like a child and open your heart to receive all that God longs to give you.

Malachi 3:1–4,23–24
Psalm 25:4–5ab,8–9,10 and 14
Luke 1:57–66

DECEMBER 24

• FOURTH SUNDAY OF ADVENT •

And coming to her, [the angel Gabriel] said,
"Hail, full of grace! The Lord is with you."
But she was greatly troubled at what was said
and pondered what sort of greeting this might be.
—LUKE 1:28–29

Last year at this time we witnessed Mary pondering all that was happening to her, and here we are again. It pays to ponder. It's an act of faith. It's an act of humility. Sometimes we're tempted to jump right into certainty when what's called for is patient wondering, letting the truth of a situation come to us rather than rushing to supply meaning to a new or surprising event. Usually when we experience awe, we simply have no words. So, when you feel the urge to grasp and explain, be quiet and ponder instead. As Mary discovered, the Holy Spirit works wonders with those who ponder.

2 Samuel 7:1–5,8b–12,14a,16
Psalm 89:2–3,4–5,27,29 (2a)
Romans 16:25–27
Luke 1:26–38

DECEMBER 25

The people who walked in darkness
have seen a great light;
upon those who dwelt in the land of gloom
a light has shone.
—ISAIAH 9:1

Merry Christmas! Today, meditate on the words and meaning of a favorite Christmas hymn. Here's one of mine: "What Child is this who, laid to rest / On Mary's lap is sleeping? / Whom angels greet with anthems sweet, / While shepherds watch are keeping? / This, this is Christ the King, / Whom shepherds guard and angels sing; / Haste, haste, to bring Him laud / The Babe, the Son of Mary."

VIGIL:
Isaiah 62:1–5
Psalm 89:4–5,16–17,27,29 (2a)
Acts 13:16–17,22–25
Matthew 1:1–25 or 1:18–25

DAWN:
Isaiah 62:11–12
Psalm 97:1,6,11–12
Titus 3:4–7
Luke 2:15–20

NIGHT:
Isaiah 9:1–6
Psalm 96:1–2,2–3,11–12,13
Titus 2:11–14
Luke 2:1–14

DAY:
Isaiah 52:7–10
Psalm 98:1,2–3,3–4,5–6 (3c)
Hebrews 1:1–6
John 1:1–18 or 1:1–5,9–14

Tuesday

DECEMBER 26

• ST. STEPHEN, THE FIRST MARTYR •

They threw him out of the city, and began to stone him.
The witnesses laid down their cloaks
at the feet of a young man named Saul.
As they were stoning Stephen, he called out,
"Lord Jesus, receive my spirit."
—ACTS 7:58–60

Like many blockbuster thrillers, just when the great threat
has been overcome and peace seemingly reigns, the
storyteller plants a hint that the struggle is not over. This
reading from Acts of the Apostles on the day after Christmas
presents such a glimpse at the future for those who will
follow the child in the manger. The battle is not yet fully
won. But we have confidence, because we, thousands of years
later, have heard the story and walked with Jesus from
manger to Calvary to the empty tomb. And so we continue
on, fortified by the child who will lead us.

Acts 6:8–10; 7:54–59
Psalm 31:3cd–4,6 and 8ab,16bc and 17
Matthew 10:17–22

Wednesday

DECEMBER 27

• ST. JOHN, APOSTLE AND EVANGELIST •

Light dawns for the just;
and gladness, for the upright of heart.
Be glad in the LORD, you just,
and give thanks to his holy name.
—PSALM 97:11–12

Before we get too far away from Christmas, spend time in
quiet, appreciating the lights and decorations in your home.
If these are minimal, light a candle and let the light bring you
gladness. If so moved, you could make a gratitude list in
writing, or just in your head. Thank God for all the blessings
received so far this season of Advent and Christmas.

1 John 1:1–4
Psalm 97:1–2,5–6,11–12
John 20:1a, 2–8

⇒ 396 ⇐

Thursday

DECEMBER 28

• THE HOLY INNOCENTS, MARTYRS •

*If we say, "We are without sin,"
we deceive ourselves, and the truth is not in us.
If we acknowledge our sins, he is faithful and just
and will forgive our sins and cleanse us
from every wrongdoing.*
—1 JOHN 1:8–9

Maybe you've heard this version of the Gospel quote: "And you shall know the truth and the truth shall set you free—but first it shall make you miserable." Seeing the truth about ourselves—especially our faults and imperfections—can feel like ripping off a bandage from a wound. But admitting the truth about ourselves is the way out of patterns of sin, ignorance of our motives, and obliviousness to the pain we cause ourselves and others. What we long for is the forgiveness that brings us to wholeness. Trust God and seek the truth about yourself. You can take it.

1 John 1:5—2:2
Psalm 124:2–3,4–5,7b–8
Matthew 2:13–18

Announce his salvation, day after day.
Tell his glory among the nations;
among all peoples, his wonderous deeds.
—PSALM 96:2B–3

I once asked a classroom of teenagers to share a story of someone who helped them grow closer to God and how that person went about it. The vast majority cited the person's example rather than their words. Perhaps the most effective way we can "tell his glory" is by walking the walk. Think about a person who inspired you to grow closer to God. Follow their example today and pass it on.

1 John 2:3–11
Psalm 96:1–2a,2b–3,5b–6
Luke 2:22–35

DECEMBER 30

They returned to Galilee,
to their own town of Nazareth.
The child grew and became strong, filled with wisdom,
and the favor of God was upon him.
—LUKE 2:39–40

Do you ever wonder what Jesus was like as a young boy, how he spent his days, what delighted him, and what struggles he might have had? Meditating on how the child Jesus grew and became strong and filled with wisdom is a good way to reenter "Ordinary Time" in the liturgical calendar. The feasts and seasons are great to heighten our awareness of key moments in Jesus' life. But so much of our lives is mundane. Pray that Jesus, Mary, and Joseph will help you see how best to grow in wisdom and grace in days to come.

1 John 2:12–17
Psalm 96:7–8a,8b–9,10
Luke 2:36–40

DECEMBER 31

Let the word of Christ dwell in you richly,
as in all wisdom you teach and admonish one another . . .
And whatever you do, in word or in deed,
do everything in the name of the Lord Jesus,
giving thanks to God the Father through him.
—COLOSSIANS 3:16–17

Today we end this daily dip into the Scripture readings of 2023. How are we to go forward? By allowing Christ to dwell in us richly. We believe in persons—Father, Son, and Holy Spirit, surely. And we believe that when two or more are gathered in Jesus' name, he is there for us. We can believe, also, in the communion of saints and the still, small voice inside of us when it's attuned to the Holy Spirit. Pray for me as I will for you. You have been a blessing to me, dear reader.

Sirach 3:2–6,12–14
Psalm 128:1–2,3,4–5
Colossians 3:12–21 or 3:12–17
Matthew 2:13–15,19–23

ABOUT THE AUTHOR

Tom McGrath, author of *Raising Faith-Filled Kids*, is a husband, father, grandfather, writer, spiritual director, parishioner, and friend. During his career, he served at Loyola Press, Truequest Communications, and *U.S. Catholic* magazine.